Harper College Library

W9-BRT-866

DATE DUE

AUG 1 8 2010			
GAYLORD			PRINTED IN U.S.A.

Reluctant Gangsters

Reluctant Gangsters
The changing face of youth crime

John Pitts

WILLAN
PUBLISHING

HARPER COLLEGE LIBRARY
PALATINE, ILLINOIS 60067

HV
9145
.P58
2008

Published by

Willan Publishing
Culmcott House
Mill Street, Uffculme
Cullompton, Devon
EX15 3AT, UK
Tel: +44(0)1884 840337
Fax: +44(0)1884 840251
e-mail: info@willanpublishing.co.uk
website: www.willanpublishing.co.uk

Published simultaneously in the USA and Canada by

Willan Publishing
c/o ISBS, 920 NE 58th Ave, Suite 300,
Portland, Oregon 97213-3786, USA
Tel: +001(0)503 287 3093
Fax: +001(0)503 280 8832
e-mail: info@isbs.com
website: www.isbs.com

© John Pitts 2008

The rights of John Pitts to be identified as the author of this book have been asserted
by him in accordance with the Copyright, Designs and Patents Act of 1988.

All rights reserved; no part of this publication may be reproduced, stored in a retrieval
system, or transmitted in any form or by any means, electronic, mechanical, photocopying,
recording or otherwise without the prior written permission of the Publishers or a licence
permitting copying in the UK issued by the Copyright Licensing Agency Ltd, Saffron
House, 6–10 Kirby Street, London EC1N 8TS.

First published 2008

ISBN   978-1-84392-365-7 paperback
       978-1-84392-366-4 hardback

British Library Cataloguing-in-Publication Data

A catalogue record for this book is available from the British Library.

Project managed by Deer Park Productions, Tavistock, Devon
Typeset by GCS, Leighton Buzzard, Bedfordshire
Printed and bound by T.J. International Ltd, Padstow, Cornwall

HARPER COLLEGE LIBRARY
PALATINE, ILLINOIS 60067

Contents

Figures and tables

Figures

Tables

About the author

John Pitts is Vauxhall Professor of Socio-legal Studies at the University of Bedfordshire. He has worked as a 'special needs' teacher, a street and club-based youth worker, a youth justice development officer, a group worker in a Young Offender Institution and a consultant to workers in youth justice, youth social work, legal professionals and the police in the UK, mainland Europe, the Russian Federation and the People's Republic of China. His research includes studies of the differential treatment of black and white offenders in the youth justice system, the violent victimisation of school students, inter-racial youth violence, the contribution of detached youth work to the life chances of socially excluded young people and violent youth gangs in London. He is editor of *Safer Communities* and his recent publications include *The New Politics of Youth Crime: Discipline or Solidarity*, Macmillan (2001) and *The Russell House Companion to Youth Justice* (with T. Bateman), Russell House Publishing (2005).

For Deborah

Compare them with the last phase of the proletariat as pictured by Marx. The proletariat, owning nothing, stripped utterly bare, would awaken at last from the nightmare of history. Entirely naked, it would have no illusions because there was nothing to support illusions and it would make a revolution without any scenario. It would need no historical script because of its merciless education in reality, and so forth. Well, here is a case of people denuded. And what's the effect of denudation, atomisation? Of course, they aren't proletarians. They're just a lumpen population. We do not know how to approach this population. We haven't even conceived that reaching it might be a problem. So there's nothing but death before it. Maybe we've already made our decision. Those who can be advanced to the middle class, let them be advanced. The rest? Well, we do our best by them. We don't have to do any more. They kill some of us. Mostly they kill themselves ...

Saul Bellow, *The Dean's December* (1982)

Acknowledgements

While I was writing this book 39 young people were either shot or stabbed to death on the streets of London in gang-related murders. One of my purposes in writing this book is to contribute in some way to the efforts of the young people, parents, local residents, politicians, police officers, and welfare, health and education professionals who are trying to stop the killing.

In writing this book I interviewed, or had conversations with, dozens of young people caught up in the violence. What they had to say was always thoughtful and I learnt something new from each of them. What I learnt from Bianca, Dexter, Haley and Leon at the Lambeth *X-it Programme*, however, changed the way I thought about the 'gang question' and, in many ways, determined the shape of this book. Similarly, my recent conversations with Zane Palmer helped me understand the idea of involuntary affiliation much more clearly. Thanks are due too, to Marcus and Anna, my in-house south London youth culture gurus, who have prevented me from committing several very embarrassing *faux pas*.

I have gained a great deal from working alongside Suzella Palmer, a talented researcher whose fieldwork on a north-west London estate, and opinions about the racial politics of the capital, have been an important influence. Marlon Campbell, Dan Briggs, Tim Hope, Shaila Mahomed, Julia Wolton, from the *X-it Programme*, and Jock Young have opened many new doors, while Cllr Lorna Campbell from Lambeth has, single-handedly, almost restored my faith in politicians. At London South Bank University I have, once again, gained enormously from my discussions with, and the opportunities provided by,

Roger Matthews. John Hagedorn from the University of Illinois at Chicago has been a great support and a trusty 'critical friend', as I have tried to understand the similarities and differences between the British and American experience. Andrew Cooper at the Tavistock Clinic has, as ever, helped me understand the psychodynamics of the sociological phenomena I am endeavouring to describe.

At the University of Bedfordshire, Tim Bateman, Fiona Factor, Steve Hallam, Ravi Kohli, Alan Marlow, Margaret Melrose, David Porteous and Jenny Pearce have helped in all sorts of ways, while the stunningly efficient Cara Senouri and Tracey Kidman have, as usual, been wonderful.

Deborah understood what I was trying to do and why I thought it was important, and this book is dedicated to her.

Chapter 1

Things have changed

Many personal troubles cannot be solved merely as troubles, but must be understood in terms of public issues – and in terms of the problems of history making. Know that the human meaning of public issues must be revealed by relating them to personal troubles – and to the problems of the individual life. Know that the problems of social science, when adequately formulated, must include both troubles and issues, both biography and history, and the range of their intricate relations. Within that range the life of the individual and the making of societies occur; and within that range the sociological imagination has its chance to make a difference in the quality of human life in our time.

C. Wright Mills (1959)

Introduction

C. Wright Mills says that the job of sociology is to turn private troubles into public issues, and that is the purpose of this book. The private troubles are, primarily, those of young people affected by violent youth gangs. The public issue is the progressive estrangement of the neighbourhoods in which they and their families live from the social, economic and political mainstream.

Gangs? What gangs?

The media and 'social commentators' have been mistakenly identifying American-style, violent, youth gangs in Britain for the last 50 years at least. Not so social scientists, however. David Downes, in his classic study of young people and crime in east London, *The Delinquent Solution* (1966), found no evidence of American-style 'youth gangs' and, over the next 30 years or so, nor did anyone else. In the mid 1990s, Peter Stelfox (1998) embarked upon a national survey for the Home Office to see if he could track them down. Although he elicited a remarkable 91.45 per cent response rate to his questionnaire, only 16 police services were able to identify gangs in their area, yielding a national total of 72. The majority of the UK gangs identified by Stelfox were composed of adult males aged between 25 and 29. Some gangs spanned a broader age range with a few gang members below the age of 16. These gangs were predominantly white, only 25 per cent had members described as 'Black Caribbean', and only 7 per cent had members who were predominantly from ethnic minority groups. This led Stelfox to conclude that:

> These figures challenge the perception that violent gangs are primarily either a youth problem or one which occurs mainly within ethnic communities. Organisationally the majority of gangs tended towards a loose structure.

This being so, we approached our study of 'violent youth gangs' in a London borough, in 2006, with a degree of scepticism and we asked our 54 interviewees these three questions:

1 What do you mean by a 'youth gang'?
2 Are there youth gangs in this area?

And if the answer to this was yes:

3 How long have they been here?

The groups our respondents described certainly sounded like violent youth gangs and they had, it seemed, been active in the area for between five and eight years. Things, our respondents believed, had changed.

Things have changed

Three 'Muslim Boys' jailed after shooting at family home

Three more members of the notorious Muslim Boys gang have been locked up after being caught with loaded guns. Stefon Thomas 23, Marlon Stubbs 25, and Sanjit Webster 20, were arrested during an investigation into a shooting outside a family home. Gunmen fired a hail of bullets at Marlon Crooks, his eight-year-old daughter, mum, grandmother, sister and brother on October 10 last year. Miraculously, they all escaped injury. Thomas and Stubbs were picked out by an eyewitness but were cleared of attempted murder by an Old Bailey jury. But a week after the shooting, Thomas was caught with a D-32 Derringer pistol and on November 3, Webster and Stubbs were arrested with a .44 calibre weapon. All three were convicted of possession of a firearm with intent to endanger life. Stubbs who has a previous conviction for raping two schoolgirls, had been cleared at the Old Bailey in September 2005 of conspiracy to murder a rival, Adrian Marriott. It was claimed Mr Marriott had been shot in the head with a machine gun in Brixton by members of the Muslim Boys gang. Stubbs and Thomas will serve at least four years before being considered for parole while Webster will serve at least three-and-a-half years. Thomas was also sentenced to six years concurrent for possession of a prohibited weapon and four years concurrent on two charges of possession of prohibited ammunition. The Old Bailey heard Marlon Crooks was attacked by a gang wearing Muslim-style head-scarves while showing his family a new BMW convertible in Condell Road, Battersea. Thomas was caught with a loaded D-32 double Derringer pistol when police spotted him in his black Mercedes on October 16 last year. Stubbs and Webster were caught in the back of a taxi while travelling from Brixton to Stratford to collect the .44 pistol on November 3 last year, the last day of the Muslim festival of Ramadan. They were overheard saying, 'When Ramadan ends the snake is going to strike,' the court heard. Thomas, of no fixed address, and Stubbs, of Ward Point, Kennington, were cleared of two charges of attempted murder and one count of possession of a firearm with intent to endanger life in relation to the shooting. (icsouthlondon.co.uk, 28 November 2006)

In 2002/2003 the police in England and Wales recorded a 36 per cent increase in gun crime, with a further 2 per cent rise recorded in 2003/2004 (Home Office/RDS 2004). In 2007, a survey by the Metropolitan Police (MPS) identified 172 youth gangs in London alone, many using firearms in furtherance of their crimes, and estimated to be responsible for 20 per cent of the youth crime in the capital and 28 knife and gun murders.

As gun crime rose, the ages of perpetrators fell. Whereas in 2003, young people under 20 constituted 16 per cent of victims of the 'black-on-black' gun crime, investigated by Operation Trident, by 2006 this had risen to 31 per cent. Bullock and Tilley (2003) found that the ages of the predominantly African-Caribbean and mixed heritage gang members involved in gun crime in south Manchester were evenly spread from their early teens to twenties: two to four at every age between 15 and 23.

In London in 2007 28 young people under the age of 20 were killed in 'gang-related' murders. Moreover, between April and November 1,237 young people were injured in gun and knife attacks: 321 were shot, 39 'seriously'; 952 were stabbed, 188 'seriously'. There were 12 armed rapes and 88 'gun-enabled' muggings (MPS 2007).

Of course, these figures are generated by the police and the Home Office and, over the period, there have been important changes in policing policy, policing practice and crime recording techniques. Nonetheless, these shifts are no mere statistical quirk and, if anything, significantly understate the problem.

Things have changed, and despite a steady decline in adult and youth crime in Britain in the past 15 years, in certain parts of our towns and cities and among certain social groups, life has become far more dangerous for children and young people. And the immediate reason for this is the proliferation of violent youth gangs and the culture that they ferment.

The research

Chapters 4 to 9 of this book are based on studies undertaken in three high-crime London boroughs, *Red*, *White* and *Blue*, between 2005 and 2008. In Red borough we mapped the number, nature, seriousness and social impact of youth gangs, interviewing over 50 respondents and interrogating the available statistical data. In White borough we evaluated a gang desistance programme, interviewed participants and peer mentors, and took evidence from professionals and volunteers working in gang-affected neighbourhoods. In Blue borough we evaluated a gang diversion programme and undertook research into street crime. Here, we interviewed young people, their parents and the professionals who worked with them. Chapter 9 also draws on a study of projects, undertaken in Anderlecht in Brussels, Belgium, Den Helder in Holland, and Palermo in Italy in 2005, that successfully reintroduced ethnic and cultural minority children and young people to education, training and employment.

Over the period, we talked to over 300 respondents: young people who were involved in gangs and others who were adversely affected by them, parents, local residents; and professionals in education, housing, criminal justice, community safety, welfare and healthcare.

Although, in Red, White and Blue boroughs, the majority of gang-involved young people were of Black, African-Caribbean, or mixed heritage, a substantial minority of white and South Asian young people were also involved. However, although ethnicity was a shaping force in local street cultures, it is clear that the violent youth gang phenomenon is not reducible to a question of race.

Glasgow has a legacy of inter-gang violence, perpetrated by White young people, that stretches back over a century. In certain parts of that city, men in their seventies and eighties still claim an affiliation to local gangs. Similarly, the violent gang conflict in Liverpool, which hit the headlines with the murder of eleven-year-old Rhys Jones in 2007, involves mainly white adolescents and young adults. Indeed, in seeking an explanation of the gang phenomenon, we have found that social class offers a more salient explanatory schema than race.

Describing gangs

We speak of describing rather than defining gangs because, while description can always be augmented by new knowledge and fresh insights, definition, by demarcating a field of study too narrowly, often restricts the scope of enquiry and lacks the flexibility to accommodate changes in the phenomenon it endeavours to illuminate. As John Hagedorn notes:

> The definition issue is hopelessly muddled, and I think misplaced. In fact, gangs, militias, 'organised crime' and other sorts of groups of armed young men are fairly transient. They are flexible forms that can take on many different shadings and usually do over their life course. (2006, personal communication)

Data gathered in Red, White and Blue boroughs suggests the following working descriptions of gangs, what we have called 'gang cultures' and 'gangland'.

When we use the term 'gang' we mean children and young people who see themselves, and are seen by others, as affiliates of a discrete, named, group with a discernible structure and a recognised territory. Affiliates seldom describe these groups as a 'gang', using terms like *crew, family, massive, posse, brerrs, man dem, cousins* or *boys*. Most young affiliates appear to be preoccupied with 'respect', usually achieved through the illicit acquisition of wealth, control over residential, drug-dealing or street-robbery territory, and the intimidation and coercion of the people who live in that territory. They are almost always in conflict with rival gangs, who wish to take over their territory and their wealth, and the police who wish to capture them. Yet, if anything, these struggles appear to strengthen the gang's identity, thus sustaining its existence.

We use the term 'gang cultures' to mean the distinctive beliefs, values, attitudes, behaviours and rituals of the gang and its affiliates, and the passive, defensive or aggressive responses elicited from unaffiliated or reluctantly affiliated young people and adults as a result of the realities of life in 'gangland'.

By 'gangland' we mean a geographical and psychological territory where the gang exerts control over the lives of both its affiliates and the unaffiliated young people and adults who reside there. This control determines what they can and cannot say, to whom they can say it, what can be done, and with whom, and in some instances who can live there and who cannot. This is territory that once belonged in the public sphere but, because it can no longer be defended, has been effectively ceded to the gangs.

The structure of this book

This book is about gangs although, as we have observed, 'gang' is a slippery term. For this reason we devote Chapter 2 to a discussion of the unresolved, and possibly irresolvable, definitional issue. In particular, we consider the contribution of mainstream American gang scholarship to gang definition because, despite its failure to make much of a dent on the youth gang problem in the USA over the past half century, its definitions of and approaches to the 'gang problem' are increasingly influential in Europe.

In Chapter 3 we consider the two main ways in which gangs, and their social and political significance, are conceptualised within contemporary British criminology. We characterise these as the *youth governance thesis* and the *risk factor paradigm*. The youth governance thesis endeavours to persuade us that contemporary anxieties about youth violence are fostered by government, the police and the media, that youth crime itself is, more or less, as it has always been, and that if we believe differently, we are in the thrall of some kind of 'catastrophist discourse'. The risk factor paradigm, by contrast, tells us that we confront a serious problem: one that is, in large part, a product of the deficiencies of individuals and their dysfunctional families. However, it fails to tell us why so few dysfunctional individuals are gang members and why a significant minority of gang affiliates suffer from few, if any, of these deficits. We therefore posit a third perspective, which we describe as a 'political economy' of gangland, one which, because it is rooted in the day-to-day realities of 'gangland', could suggest new directions for intervention with gangs.

In Chapter 4 we argue that 'gangland' is, in large part, a product of the responses of a succession of neo-liberal governments to what is sometimes described as economic and cultural globalisation. It is their decisions, in the spheres of housing, employment, social security, education, and crime and justice, we argue, that have pushed some poor young families to the social margins, and beyond, and have created in Britain, for the first time in over 100 years, areas that are estranged from the social and economic mainstream and the body politic.

In Chapter 5 we examine the changes in organised crime, street-corner crime and the international drugs trade that, we argue, have precipitated the forms of violent youth crime described in this book.

Chapter 6 explores the diverse components of street or gang culture and the ways in which it comes to structure the world-view of gang-affiliated children and young people and the lives of those who live in gang-affected neighbourhoods.

In Chapter 7 we explore the issue of gang affiliation, arguing that the idea of 'gang membership' is too restrictive a way of looking at the nature of gang affiliation and the motivations of those who become involved with them. We argue that many young people are involved with gangs as a strategy for keeping themselves as safe as they can in a highly dangerous situation and that, ultimately, this renders the task of ascribing responsibility for gang-related violence and offending, in both criminological theory and the law, extremely difficult.

Chapter 8 traces the impact of violent youth gangs on the people who have the grave misfortune to live in 'gangland'.

In Chapter 9 we think about what it would take, at the levels of politics, policy, administration and practice, for the five objectives of the government's *Every Child Matters* initiative in gangland to be realised: that every child should *Be healthy, Stay safe, Enjoy and achieve, Make a positive contribution* and *Achieve economic well-being.*

Chapter 2

The obscure object of investigation

The only thing we knew for sure about Henry Porter is that his name wasn't Henry Porter.
Bob Dylan and Sam Shepard, *Brownsville Girl* (1986)

Categorical imperatives

The Argentinian novelist and critic Jorge Luis Borges (1993) writes of a Chinese encyclopaedia, *The Celestial Empire of Benevolent Knowledge*, in which animals are divided into:

(a) those that belong to the Emperor; (b) embalmed ones; (c) those that are trained; (d) suckling pigs: (e) mermaids; (f) fabulous ones; (g) stray dogs; (h) those that are included in this classification; (i) those that tremble as if they were mad; (j) innumerable ones; (k) those drawn with a very fine camel's hair brush; (l) et cetera; (m) those that have broken the flower vase; (n) those that at a distance resemble flies.

This attempt to marshal the infinite variety of categorical possibilities into a coherent taxonomy may appear eccentric today, but it probably made sense to its fifth-century BC readership. Nonetheless, one suspects that it was shaped in no small part by the idiosyncratic preoccupations of its author. Likewise, the diverse concerns of those who have studied youth gangs mean that what they are looking at sometimes becomes conflated with what they are looking for.

Many classic 'gang studies' are only incidentally concerned with gangs, presenting them as an instance, a function, a product, an effect, or evidence for the existence of, the social, cultural, psychological, political or economic phenomena or processes that are the author's principal concern.

For the Chicago School (Park *et al.* 1925; Shaw and McKay 1942), the street gang is an inevitable corollary of the 'social disorganisation' evident, to them, in the run-down migrant neighbourhoods from which the gangs are drawn. For Zorbaugh (1929), however, the gang's significance resides in its role as a training ground for organised crime. Whereas Bloch and Neiderhoffer's gang (1958) provides the sustained peer support necessary to create a pathway to adulthood for disadvantaged adolescents, Yablonsky's violent gang (1962) coalesces, sporadically, around a hard core of paranoiac 'sociopaths', bent upon violence. Although it is evident to Hirschi (1969) that gang crime, like all other crime, emanates from an absence of self-control, the gang members in Cloward and Ohlin's (1960) 'organised slum' reveal exemplary restraint as they quietly develop their illicit opportunity structures.

The variety of sometimes contradictory perspectives developed by the anthropologists, criminologists, economists, game-show hosts, journalists, police officers, political activists, psychologists, psychotherapists and sociologists who have studied gangs have made the task of devising a coherent definition of the gang, its dimensions and its significance, difficult.

This is, as we note in Chapter 4, one of the reasons why earlier, 'appreciative' studies of the gang did not dwell for long on the questions of definition that now absorb so much of the time and energy of gang scholars. But, as we have also noted, the other reason is that definition, by its very nature, restricts the focus of enquiry, whereas description and explanation imposes no such limits, being bounded only by the intellectual and imaginative powers of the describer and explainer.

The correctional turn

With the advent of crack cocaine and structural youth unemployment in the 1980s, the number of US street gangs increased dramatically. And so too did the numbers of people studying gangs. However, whereas earlier, 'appreciative' studies proceeded from an empathetic understanding of the plight of gang-involved young people, the lavishly funded gang scholarship that emerged in the radically changed political climate of the last quarter of the twentieth century was decidedly 'correctional', bent upon neutralising the threat they posed to the law-abiding majority. They took the form of:

- Studies of the behavioural characteristics of (usually apprehended) gang members, which endeavoured to identify the 'risk factors' associated with gang involvement in order to develop predictive instruments to facilitate early intervention with 'gang-prone' children and young people.

- Longitudinal studies of randomly selected populations of children and young people, designed to establish the life events and personal characteristics that presage gang involvement.

- Studies of the frequency and nature of offending by gang-involved and non-gang-involved children and young people.

- Self-report studies, often taking the form of surveys, usually conducted in schools, which aimed to establish the prevalence of gang involvement in particular populations or locales.

- Anthropological studies of the signs and symbols, the iconography, and rituals of gang membership, designed to enable early recognition and intervention.

However, as David Matza (1969: 17) writes:

> When deviant phenomena are seen and studied from the correctional perspective, the possibility of 'losing the phenomenon' – reducing it to what it is not – is heightened. The purpose of ridding ourselves of the phenomenon manifests itself most clearly in the overwhelming contemporary concern with questions of causation or 'etiology'. The phenomenon itself receives only cursory attention. The ultimate purpose of liquidation is reflected in this highly disproportionate division of attention between description and explanation ... Why bother with detailed and subtle description? The task before us, in the correctional perspective, is to get at the root causes in order to remove their product.

This shift towards correctionalism was a fateful one for both public policy and the social sciences. Critics of the correctional turn, like Joan Moore (1991), James Short (1997) and John Hagedorn (1998), have argued that the central place accorded to crime in the mainstream gang studies of this period projects too simplistic a picture of the motivations of gang members and too narrow a definition of the gang. However, the tide had turned and now scholarly research was part of the fight against gangs, which was, in turn, part and parcel of Ronald Reagan's War On Drugs.

Definition or description

In the shift away from a social science that endeavoured to understand and explain, to one that aimed to quantify, qualify and correct, the problem of definition was accorded a central place. The impetus to define derives from:

1 The desire to demarcate a discrete field of academic endeavour by placing limits upon the range of phenomena that may be regarded as proper objects of scientific investigation.

2 The desire to develop legal and administrative instruments with which to identify, and then contain, suppress or eradicate, problematic social groups or group behaviours.

3 The desire to conjoin 1 and 2 above.

Thus, like many other definitions devised in this period, Walter B. Miller's (1982) widely influential, scholarly definition of the gang has strong echoes of statutory definitions:

> A group of recurrently associating individuals with identifiable leadership and internal organisation, identifying with or claiming control over territory in the community, and engaging either individually or collectively in violent or other forms of illegal behaviour.

Similarly, the Chicago Municipal Criminal Code describes the gang as:

> Any ongoing organisation, association in fact or group of three or more persons, whether formal or informal, having as one of its substantial activities the commission of criminal gang activity, and whose ... members individually or collectively engage in or have engaged in a pattern of criminal gang activity.

What these gang definitions lack, however, is what Thrasher (1929), in his early studies, came to view as the gang's defining feature, the essential hermetic that binds it together: 'conflict'. To ignore the fact that both gang-affiliated and non-affiliated young people in gang-affected neighbourhoods are under threat from their own and rival gangs, and must therefore live constantly in a state of preparedness for action, forming such strategic partnerships as they can to protect themselves from gang violence is, as we shall argue, a fateful oversight.

Definitional entrepreneurism

Malcolm Klein (2001), the Californian architect of *Eurogang*, has attempted to extend the scope and reach of gang definitions by elaborating a five-point typology (see Figure 2.1). He argues that this level of specificity is necessary because, with the 'globalisation' of the gang phenomenon in the 1980s and 1990s, the involvement of youth gangs in far more serious, usually drug-related, crime and the consequent links they have forged with organised criminal networks, most earlier definitions fail to grasp the scope and complexity of the contemporary gang phenomenon.

He maintains that, for these reasons, we are encountering similar gang forms in both the USA and Europe. However, Klein's *traditional* and *neo-traditional* gangs (see Figure 2.1 below) presume a 'tradition' which is peculiarly North American. As for his *compressed, collective* and *speciality* gangs, it is difficult to see why they are described as 'gangs' at all. While his *compressed* and *collective* gangs lack structure and the *distinguishing characteristics of traditional and neo-traditional gangs,* the *speciality* gang, being 'formless', is by definition unrecognisable as a gang.

Klein's response to European scepticism about the relevance of these categories is to argue that Europeans have tended to view the American gang as a far more structured and durable entity than it actually is, and were they to abandon this misapprehension they would soon discover a plethora of youth gangs in Europe (Klein 2001). However, were European scholars to adopt Klein's categories, this would, at a stroke, precipitate a massive increase in the European gang population. Although this would open up many new research opportunities for gang scholars, it risks criminalising vast swathes of European young people who are simply 'hanging out' together.

The traditional gang. Has usually been in existence for 20 plus years. It has a large membership and a wide age range and almost always claims territory (turf/'hood/barrio). It is able to regenerate itself and is composed of sub-groups that are often determined by age (seniors/juniors) but sometimes by neighbourhood.

The neo-traditonal gang. Similar to the traditional gang but has been in existence for a shorter period (less than ten years). It usually contains sub-groups based on age or area but encompasses a smaller age range. It claims and defends territory like a traditional gang.

The compressed gang. Small (less than 50 members). It has no sub-groups, a narrow age range and has been in existence for only a few years.

The collective gang. Like the compressed gang but bigger with a wider age range but no sub-groups. It is a 'shapeless mass' of adolescent and young adult members that has not developed the distinguishing characteristics of traditional and neo-traditional gangs.

The speciality gang. Narrowly focused on a few offence types. Its major focus is criminal rather than social. It is small (less than 50 members), has a narrow age range and is less than ten years old. Its territory is either residential or based on opportunities for particular forms of crime.

Figure 2.1 Malcolm Klein's five-point typology of street gangs

In Europe, this kind of definitional entrepreneurism has met with some resistance. Although the definition developed by the European arm of Eurogang places a similar emphasis upon *criminality, durability, territoriality* and *structure*, in its efforts to define a distinctively European 'gang' it eventually chose to avoid the word 'gang' altogether for fear of inadvertently stigmatising young people and sparking a 'moral panic'. What emerges, however, is an insipid mishmash that raises far more questions than it answers:

> Any durable street-oriented youth group whose involvement in illegal acts is part of their identity.

This points to the difficulty of translating terms with a particular connotation in one national culture into the language of another. This is nowhere more evident than in the UK.

Lost in translation

The old adage that Britain and the USA are two nations divided by a common language holds true in the area of youthful misbehaviour. Whereas in the USA the term 'gang' continues to enjoy universal currency, in Britain until the last decade of the twentieth century the term 'gang', as a description of groups of young people on the streets, had more or less fallen into abeyance. 'Gang' was used fairly commonly from the late nineteenth to the mid twentieth century, initially describing groups of rowdy adolescents (Pearson 1984), but latterly, adult-organised crime groups like the race-track gangs portrayed by Graham Greene in *Brighton Rock* (1947) and groups of London gangsters like the Krays and the Richardsons (Hobbs 1988, 2001). In twentieth-century Britain, the term 'gang' has had its widest currency in primary school playgrounds, where younger children have used it to describe their friendship groups.

In Britain, for most of the twentieth century, there was no generic term to describe groups of rowdy adolescents. Terminology varied from town to town, region to region and time to time. London had its 'yobs', 'geezers' and 'hounds', Liverpool its 'scallies' and Newcastle-upon-Tyne its 'stoats'. Some working-class neighbourhoods had their 'boys', who would periodically engage in set-piece battles with 'boys' from other, similar, neighbourhoods. From the 1970s, areas of African-Caribbean settlement in the major cities also had their 'posses'. But as a succession of British social scientists have observed, these were loosely structured groupings whose brawls, petty crime and disorderly conduct was occasional, and largely incidental, to the developmental processes they fostered and the solidarity they engendered (Willmott 1966; Downes 1966; Fyvel 1969; Patrick 1973; Parker 1974; Hall and Jefferson 1975; Pearson and Mungham 1976; Corrigan 1979; Pryce 1979).

As working-class geographies were transformed by de-industrialisation and migration in the 1970s (Hall and Jefferson 1975), some of these neighbourhood groupings mutated into more broadly based adversarial networks linked with the major football clubs (Taylor and Taylor 1971, Marsh and Frosdick 1978; Murphy *et al.* 1990). Over time, factions within these networks coalesced into small, relatively tightly organised, avowedly violent, groups of older adolescents and young adults; like West Ham's Intercity Firm, Birmingham City's Zulu Warriors and Milwall FC. These football 'firms' were the closest domestic equivalent to the US fighting gang that we were to witness in Britain until the very end of the twentieth century.

But most of these rowdy, pugnacious, working-class boys were also involved in the succession of popular 'youth movements' or 'youth subcultures' that emerged in Britain from the 1950s, involving hundreds of thousands of young people (Hall and Jefferson 1975). These Teddy boys, mods, ravers, skinheads, rude boys, greasers, glam rockers, punks and goths, and their many derivatives, demarcated new spaces, places and personas for working-class young people and were peculiarly British, having no indigenous North American counterparts.

And then there were gangs, characterised by *criminality, durability, territoriality, structure* and, importantly, *conflict*. These groups of young people, who appeared in London, Birmingham and Manchester in the final years of the twentieth century, fighting and sometimes killing one another for domination of crack cocaine markets, marked a significant break with the youth subcultures of the past. And to British eyes, they looked like something that had escaped from the North American ghetto rather than the home-grown cultural phenomenon they were.

'Group offending'

Curiously for a government that, since 1997, has consistently exploited fear of youth crime for electoral advantage (Pitts 2003), the advent of armed youth gangs in the major cities evoked a remarkably muted response. A report for the Youth Justice Board (2007) reflects this reticence, and in their introduction the authors are at pains to emphasise that the 'gang' is, essentially, just another kind of peer group; that group offending is a common form of youth crime; that many non-offending young people adopt a gangster 'style'; and, somewhat more contentiously, that although public anxiety may have grown, there is no evidence that group offending has increased. They also point to the dangers of talking-up 'gangs':

> Some commentators caution against the use of the term 'gang' in relation to young people since this may lend spurious glamour to the minor forms of delinquency committed by groups, and

actively encourage them to become involved in more serious offending.

In this vein, the report finds a striking degree of consensus among youth justice practitioners about the indiscriminate use of the term 'gang' and its likely consequences in terms of the self-perceptions of their hapless charges.

The authors observe that, inasmuch as they exist, 'gangs' tend to be the preserve of young adults rather than the 10–18-year-olds involved with Youth Offending Teams. Indeed, were we to stop reading the report at this point we might conclude that the furore surrounding youth gangs has all been a storm in a teacup and that, *à la* 1960's 'labelling theory', the greatest danger lies in talking about them.

However, a few paragraphs later we learn that gangs do actually exist in three of the five urban research sites where fieldwork was undertaken; that they are characterised by the intensity and seriousness of the offending of their members; that they do, in fact, involve children and young people supervised by Youth Offending Teams; that they also involve older adolescents and young adults and are often linked into adult criminal networks that control local drug markets. Moreover, they are also involved in violence and this violence sometimes involves the use of firearms.

This contradictory account reflects the ambivalence of British policy-makers and academics and it leads to the kind of clumsy, decontextualised circumlocution adopted by the British Home Office (2006) in its attempt to come to terms with the new British 'youth gang':

> Young people (who) spend time in groups of three or more. The group spends a lot of time in public places. The group has existed for 3 months or more. The group has engaged in delinquency or criminal behaviour together in the last 12 months. The group has at least one structural feature (a name, an area or a leader).

This definition is fraught with difficulties. For a start, 'delinquency' is a contested term, now largely abandoned by British criminology because of its essentialist connotations. Youth offending is, overwhelmingly, perpetrated by groups of young people and is, therefore, statistically 'normal': self-report studies consistently show that between 40 per cent and 98 per cent of adolescents admit to having broken the law in the preceding 12 months (Belson 1977; Rutter and Giller 1983; Anderson *et al.* 1994), as do around 60 per cent of middle class adults (Karstedt and Farrall 2007). Most adolescents regularly spend time outside the home in groups of three or more. These are known as 'peer groups' and they are a more or less universal, innocuous and desirable social phenomenon (Ryan 2001). It is, moreover, in the nature of such groups that they persist over time and occupy some geographical space. As a result, far from quelling public anxiety, taken seriously (which hopefully it is not) this definition would suggest that most of Britain's 10 to 18-year-olds may well be gang members.

Contextualised definitions

More usefully, the definition devised by UK scholars, Simon Hallsworth and Tara Young (2004) doesn't duck the gang issue, acknowledging that things have changed, while resisting the definitional entrepreneurism of Klein, the inadvertent 'net-widening' of Eurogang and the vagueness of the British Home Office. Their's resembles earlier US definitions, developed in the shadow of the law, but it also distinguishes the gang from other 'urban collectivities', thus providing the context that is absent in most US gang scholarship (see Figure 2.2).

An erroneous interpretation of Hallsworth and Young's schema, one that has gained currency among some practitioners, is that it presents a continuum in which the peer group is a threshold or springboard to gang involvement. However, as developmental psychology teaches,

The peer group: A small, unorganised, transient grouping occupying the same space with a common history. Crime is not integral to their self-definition.

The gang: A relatively durable, predominantly street-based group of young people who see themselves (and are seen by others) as a discernible group for whom crime and violence is integral to the group's identity.

The organised criminal group: Members are professionally involved in crime for personal gain, operating almost exclusively in the 'grey' or illegal marketplace.

Figure 2.2 Hallsworth and Young's three-point typology of urban collectivities

the adolescent peer group is ubiquitous and normal whereas youth gangs are uncommon and extraordinary.

And this demonstrates the importance of contextualising the 'youth gang' and recognising its peculiarity and its rarity. The definitions developed by Robert Gordon, a British academic working in Canada, succeed in offering a nuanced differentiation between a range of youth groupings, all of which are sometimes colloquially described as gangs (see Figure 2.3).

Youth movements. Social movements characterised by a distinctive mode of dress or other bodily adornments, a leisure-time preference, and other distinguishing features (e.g. punk rockers).

Youth groups. Comprised of small clusters of young people who hang out together in public places such as shopping centres.

Criminal groups. Small clusters of friends who band together, usually for a short period of time, to commit crime primarily for financial gain and may contain young and not so young adults as well.

Wannabe groups. Include young people who band together in a loosely structured group primarily to engage in spontaneous social activity and exciting, impulsive, criminal activity including collective violence against other groups of youths. Wannabes will often claim 'gang' territory and adopt 'gang-style' identifying markers of some kind.

Street gangs. Groups of young people and young adults who band together to form a semi-structured organisation, the primary purpose of which is to engage in planned and profitable criminal behaviour or organised violence against rival street gangs. They tend to be less visible but more permanent than other groups.

Criminal business organisations. Groups that exhibit a formal structure and a high degree of sophistication. They are composed mainly of adults and engage in criminal activity primarily for economic reasons and almost invariably maintain a low profile. Thus while they may have a name, they are rarely visible.

Figure 2.3 Robert Gordon's six-point typology of youth groupings

What Gordon's Vancouver-based work also suggests is that definitions may need to be specific to particular places, times or groups if they are to be useful.

Location, location, location

The quest for a generic definition of the gang is constrained by the reality that in any given neighbourhood, the character of gangs will be determined by local histories and contemporary contingencies. Although we may start out with a working definition of the gang derived from the scholarly literature, we will need to modify, extend and sometimes abandon this if we are to gain a sufficiently nuanced picture. Groups described as gangs range from the relatively innocuous to the highly dangerous and we need ways of assessing both their nature and their potential threat. If we are social scientists, we need to understand the specificity of local gangs in order to produce an accurate representation of them. If we are policy-makers or practitioners we need to ensure that the interventions we plan are attuned to the realities and the risks.

Mapping the gangs in Red borough

These were our objectives in the analysis of the gangs in Red borough undertaken in early 2007. The information on which this analysis is based derives from offending data held by the police and Youth Offending Teams, information from the CRIS police intelligence system and interviews with gang-involved and gang-affected young people, welfare, criminal justice and education professionals and local residents.

This analysis gives a brief description of each gang, including its *'severity score'*, which is based on the Metropolitan Police harm assessment scoring scale (MPS 2006, see Table 2.1). The score is calculated from the maximum sentence length for offences committed by gang members. The scores for Red borough gangs (see Table 2.2) are arrived at on the basis of crimes proven to have been committed by gang members as part and parcel of gang activity or crimes where there is a strong suspicion among professionals closely involved with the gangs, and their members, that a particular offence has been committed by them. On this basis, six of the 13 gangs identified in Red borough appeared to be causing a high level of harm (a high

Table 2.1.   Metropolitan Police Harm Assessment Scale

Crime type	Score/ Sentence
Possession/use of drugs	7
Supply of drugs	25
Disorder (affray)	3
Low level assault (ABH)	5
Serious assault (GBH)	25
Kidnap	25
Murder/manslaughter	25
Possession/use of knife	4
Possession/use of firearms	25
Vehicle crime (TWOC)	.5
Burglary/theft (no violence)	14
Robbery/street crime	25
Fraud (includes money laundering)	14
Criminal damage (£500–£5,000	.25
Graffiti/tagging (criminal damage)	.25
Anti-social behaviour	0

level of harm equates with the commission of serious assaults, rape, kidnapping, attempted murder and murder).

Causeway Gang (severity score 198)

The Causeway Gang has been in existence for many years. Unlike the newer gangs, membership is drawn from across the borough and beyond. The gang consists of around 30–40 people and is controlled by one of the four Red borough crime families. The Elders, drawn from the S***** family and their associates, are aged 21–28. They dominate the drugs business in Red borough and have links into several of London's most dangerous gangs/crews, most notably in Hackney, Tottenham, Haringey and Harlesden. They are involved in a wide range of serious crimes. The Youngers, aged 12–18, are also drawn from the S***** family and their associates. They are prolific violent street robbers. The Causeway Gang has been described as the 'ruling street force' in Red borough. The Causeway Youngers are in conflict with the Cromwell Close Youngers (aged 10–22) and are in an alliance with Abbots Court. Members of the Causeway Gang were recently involved in a confrontation in Court with the Cromwell Close Gang in which armed 'reinforcements' were called up from the

Table 2.2. Red borough youth gangs ranked on the Metropolitan Police Harm Assessment Scale

Causeway Gang	198 (maximum score)
Puff City	198 (maximum score)
Abbots Court	169
Red African Devils	150 (est.)
Cruise	145.25
Border/Monserrat	120
Tintern	100
Asian Auto Takeaway Inc.	78
Barrier Boys	45.5
Russian/Lithuanian/Polish Gangs	40+ (est.)
Burnell Heath Gang	35
New World Order	28
Walford Overground Commuters	25+ (est.)

Causeway estate. It is said that the Causeway Gang is responsible for several recent 'hits' but this has not been proven.

Puff City (severity score 198)

Puff City comprises the Wordsworth Hall Man Dem, the Cromwell Close Gang, the Keats Close Boys, the Shelley Fam and the Byron Crew and has around 100 members. Ultimate control of Puff City is in the hands of families of adult gangsters (aged 26–40). Puff City is named after a real person, but whoever assumes control becomes known as 'Puff'. Cromwell Close has no Elders at present because they are all in jail. The Cromwell Close Youngers are aged 10–22. The Elders in the Wordsworth Hall Man Dem are particularly prolific criminals and are responsible for all of the offences listed. The Keats Close Boys and Wordsworth Hall Elders are aged 24–40 and the Youngers 14-18. Puff City is in conflict with the Causeway Gang.

Abbots Court (severity score 169)

The Abbots Court Gang is said to have been in existence for only three years and is composed of 20–30 young people in two factions: the Youngers and the Elders. Abbots Court has family links with the Keats Close Boys via the M******* family. It is allied with and has family links into the Causeway Gang and is in conflict with the Cromwell Close Gang. It is said that the Abbots Court Gang will 'do anything'.

Red African Devils (severity score 150)

There is some dispute about the Red African Devils, who may be a local subset of a pan-London crew known as the Black African Devils, composed of young Somalis, many of whom were originally unaccompanied asylum seekers, who are involved in violent street crime across the capital. The half-dozen young people in question live on the King's Road and are allegedly involved in violent street crime. They are said to be particularly dangerous because, unlike most street robbers, they have a tendency to use their knives prior to demanding their victim's possessions.

Cruise (severity score 145.25)

Cruise is a new gang and comprises 30–40 young people aged between 14 and 17 from Larkin Terrace, Heaney Street, Auden Street and Owen Road. Many of them know one another from their time at Worcester School. This area is in the top 5 per cent of the most deprived neighbourhoods in the country (Red Borough C&D Audit 2004). It is said that they separated themselves from other gangs when the anti-social behaviour and inter-gang conflict was 'getting out of hand'. One part of Cruise is linked to Abbots Court, while another has links with Cromwell Close even though Cromwell Close is in conflict with Causeway, and Abbots Court is in an alliance with them. It is said that Cruise was responsible for a recent firearms murder.

Border/Monserrat (severity score 120)

The Border gang has been in existence for many years but Border/Monserrat is more recent, composed of two groups: Youngers aged 12–15 and Elders aged 18–22, totalling around 20–30 young people. Eight of the Elders are originally from Monserrat, which they left as children following the eruption of the volcano that devastated the island. The group is located in Castle Gardens, an area vacated by the Causeway Gang some time ago when the 'heat was on'. The group is said to be 'very quiet'. They don't 'hang out' and they 'don't do street business', partly because youth facilities in the area are good. They are, however, said to be 'into everything' and a recent 'supply shooting' is believed to have been perpetrated by them. They have links into the North Star Gang in Hackney. Border/Monserrat is not in conflict with other gangs but has an alliance with Cromwell Close.

Tintern (severity score 100)

Tintern is a well-established local criminal gang, controlled by the B**** brothers, and located on the border of an adjacent borough, where they do most of their 'business'. The age of members ranges from as young as 10 to over 30. It is said that Tintern has around 30 members. In recent times, the gang has been implicated in several stabbings and the shooting of a police officer. The Tintern gang is said to have links into gangs in two adjacent boroughs.

Asian Auto Takeaway Inc. (severity score 78)

This is a group of around 15 South Asian young men aged 16–20, five of whom are currently in jail. They work for an older man, M***** S*****, whose 'day job' is property development and estate agency. M***** S***** owns a £2 million house in the suburbs. The young men target the owners of high-value vehicles, following them to their homes. Later they break in and steal the keys, and the cars. They receive a few hundred pounds for each job. M***** S***** ships the cars out to Pakistan, Dubai and Poland. This and his other nefarious businesses, and their personnel, are protected from other gangs in the borough by a large group of notoriously violent adolescents and young adults of Pakistani origin who operate in several adjacent boroughs.

Barrier Boys (severity score 45.5)

The Barrier Boys have been in existence for about three years. The 10–20 members are aged 15–18 and hang out at a steel barrier across Carter Lane, a side street near a college of further education, and 'tax' and harass young people who want to come by. They specialise in anti-social behaviour, low-level robbery and sexual harassment. They use, and may supply, 'soft drugs'.

Russian/Lithuanian/Polish Gangs (severity score 40+)

These groups reside on the other side of the King's Road from the

Red African Devils and are allegedly involved in pimping Eastern European prostitutes, drug sales and possibly people-trafficking as well. They have recruited half a dozen African Caribbean boys aged between 13 and 16 to distribute the drugs and pimp for the women.

Burnell Heath Gang (severity score 35)

The Burnell Heath Gang has existed for between three and five years and is composed of five to ten young people aged 15–18, three of whom are 'looked after' by the local authority in a local children's home. They engage in street robbery, using knives as a threat, and are involved in the drink-related disorder for which Burnell Heath is currently a 'hot spot' (there is a dispersal order in operation).

New World Order (severity score 28)

A group of half a dozen men in their twenties, who are said to be 'very friendly', possibly due to their prolific consumption (and suspected supply) of soft drugs. They are not violent and not obviously affiliated to any other gang or crew.

Walford Overground Commuters (severity score 25+)

Over the past two years this group of five to ten young people from an adjacent borough, aged 12–18 have been commuting in to undertake street robberies in Burnell Heath where they believe the pickings are better because local residents appear to be well off.

The gangs of Red borough

The six-point typology in Figure 2.4 endeavours to capture the nature, variety and level of threat posed by the gangs of Red borough. Taken together with the severity scores, it is designed to provide a basis for the development of a proportionate response. For example, although the Causeway Gang and the Barrier Boys see themselves, and are seen, as gangs, in terms of the threat they pose they might as well come from different planets, and if we are to intervene intelligently we need to know this.

Definition	Description	Membership
The articulated super gang	A local, originally familial, grouping, with a long history of involvement in organised crime, that moved into the drugs business in the 1990s. It is 'institutionalised', having a broad age range and the ability to regenerate itself. Its sub-groups are determined by age (Tinys/Youngers/Elders) role (Shotters/Soldiers) and location/territory. It has horizontal links into, and does 'business' with, other gangs, both within and beyond the borough. It has vertical links upwards into higher echelon organised crime and downwards to its retailers, the Shotters, and the Youngers/Soldiers who protect gang territory and gang business. Supporting themselves through street crime, Youngers/Soldiers may, in turn, delegate tasks to Tinys, Girlfriends or aspirant Wannabees who hover on the margins of the gang. The Super Gang has a name, and claims both residential and drug-dealing territory (although senior members may be widely dispersed) and it exerts a high level of control over these neighbourhoods, drawing reluctant gangsters into the fold.	Causeway Puff City Tintern Border/Monserrat
The segmented street gang	A relatively durable, predominantly street-based group of young people who see themselves (and are seen by others) as a discernible group. Crime and violence are integral to the group's identity. It has sub-groups defined by age but is less than ten years old. It has a name and its territory is either residential or based on opportunities for particular forms of crime.	Abbots Court
The new street gang	New, relatively small, has a narrow age range and no sub-groups. Members see themselves (and are seen by others) as a discernible group	Cruise

Type	Description	Examples
The criminal youth group	and crime and violence are integral to its identity. It has a name, and claims both residential and drug-dealing territory. Its *raison d'être* is primarily criminal rather than social and it is narrowly focused on a few offence types. It is small, recent and has a narrow age range. Its territory is either residential or based on opportunities for particular forms of crime.	New World Order Walford Overground Commuters Red African Devils
The wannabes	Wannabes have not developed the structural characteristics of traditional gangs. They have a narrow age range and high turnover. Although wannabes may assume the trappings of street gangs, insignia, street names, etc. and lay claim to territory, they are loosely structured groups, engaging in spontaneous social activity and impulsive criminal activity, including collective violence against other groups of youths.	Barrier Boys Burnell Heath
The middle level international criminal business organisation	Composed primarily of adults and may well be the London end of an international crime network. They also engage in street-level drug-dealing, using local adolescents to undertake deliveries. They maintain a low profile	Asian Auto Takeaway Inc. Russian/ Lithuanian/Polish Gangs

Figure 2.4 A six-point typology of Red borough gangs

Proliferation and change

However, the problem with typologies is that they do not tell us how or why violent youth gangs come into being in the first place, why they persist, why they change over time, the role they play in the lives of their members and their impact on the neighbourhoods in which they are located. These questions are discussed in the following chapters.

Chapter 3

Thinking about gangs

Simon (1997) has argued that the salience of law and order in the United States is such that its citizens are continually governing themselves through their reaction to crime. Arguably, more accurately, it is the constellation of images thrown up by youth, disorder and crime that provide the basis of contemporary contexts of governance.

Muncie and Hughes (2002)

There were too few White gang members to study, but among African American boys, first gang entry was predicted prospectively by both baseline conduct disorder (CD) behaviors and increasing levels of CD behaviors prior to gang entry. This suggests that gang entry may be a further developmental step for some boys who are already on a trajectory of worsening antisocial behavior. Having friends prior to gang entry who engaged in aggressive delinquency increased the risk of gang entry further, but only during early adolescence. Family income and parental supervision also independently predicted gang entry, but the direction of their influences depended on the youth's age.

Lahey et al. (1999)

Many of today's gangs are an institutionalised bricolage of illicit enterprise, social athletic club, patron to the poor, employment agency for youth, substitute family, and nationalist community, or militant organisation. This institutionalisation of gangs, as we have seen, has a long Chicago tradition. However, Black gangs differ from their early Irish and Italian relatives in their social exclusion within segregated ghettoes and in their inability to manipulate the levers of real power.

Hagedorn (2007)

This chapter considers two, currently influential, accounts of the youth gang proffered by social scientists, each of which tells a different story about their nature and genesis, and offers a third account rooted in the day-to-day realities of life in the gang.

Crime-averse criminologies: the governance thesis

It is not uncommon for criminal justice and social welfare professionals to attend conferences and training events at which they are assured by a speaker that the widespread concern about 'youth gangs' is, in large part, a fabrication of a racist media, or the work of a manipulative government bent on exploiting the fear of crime for its own ends.

In what Ulrich Beck (1992) characterises as the 'risk society', the argument runs, it is the anxieties, rather than the ideals, of electors and those who wish to be elected by them that drive the political process. And, in a situation where the voters who make the difference are disproportionately middle-aged, white and relatively prosperous, it comes as no surprise that the targets of governmental demonisation are disproportionately non-white, non-prosperous and non-young (Pitts 2003). Thus, governmental assessments of the threat of crime are invariably exaggerated by a political elite bent on concentrating more power in the hands of the state and, in so doing, redefining the powers of government, the role of families and schools, and the place of the individual in society (Simon 2007). This is a process that Simon (2007) describes as 'Governing through Crime, a response to risk and fear spun out of control, a response that erodes social trust and, with it, the very scaffolding of a 'free' society.'

In this account, changes in governmental crime control strategies are explained in terms of the advanced liberal *Zeitgeist* in which anxieties precipitated by accelerating social, economic and cultural change, and amplified by government, via a sensation-seeking media, are projected onto criminalised 'others'. It follows that the threat posed by crime is always exaggerated and governmental responses are almost invariably disproportionate. Yet, in some of our poorest neighbourhoods, some residents, particularly if they are black, Asian or young single parents, live in constant fear of harassment and violent victimisation. Have they misunderstood the problem? To suggest that crime is being exploited by politicians and a rapacious criminal justice system, and spun by a sensationalist media, is not the same as saying that public anxiety is necessarily baseless, nor that crime itself is unproblematic.

Could both be true?

Of course, the 'governmentality thesis' is not without substance. From 1997 the Blair government blatantly exploited fear of crime in general, and youth crime and disorder in particular, as a means of attracting, and then holding together, a new 'post-political', centre-left, constituency (Pitts 2003). As a result, the crime prevention, crime control, community safety, anti-social behaviour and youth justice industries of England and Wales have grown exponentially, drawing into their orbit ever larger numbers of less problematic children and young people on the pretext of preventing some ill-defined future wrongdoing. As Jane Mooney and Jock Young (2007) have argued, faced with a falling crime rate, the Blair government was only able to sustain the 'law and order' crusade, upon which it had based its claims to competence, by criminalising previously lawful forms of low-level social deviance through its 'anti-social behaviour' legislation. However, the desired political pay-off of this strategy was that 'Middle England' would develop confidence in New Labour's capacity to 'stop the rot', and return us to an era of moral continence, due deference and civility (Pitts 2003).

However, it was one thing to ramp up public concern about relatively innocuous incivilities, but quite another to explain the sudden explosion of serious, and apparently unstoppable, armed youth violence on the streets that a decade of New Labour's social, educational, employment, equalities and criminal justice policies should have obviated. Rather than exploiting this new phenomenon as yet another form of disorder to be eradicated, another group of undesirables to be disciplined, another example of what happens when the balance between rights and responsibilities goes out of kilter, New Labour under Gordon Brown promptly launched 'public reassurance' as a major new strand of criminal justice policy.

Public reassurance

The gang problem took New Labour by surprise. But when they did eventually grasp what was going on in Moss Side, Handsworth and on the streets of east and south-east London, New Labour's law and order crusade stopped dead in its tracks.

Despite a belief in the upper echelons of the police service that two of the most pressing problems they face are armed youth gangs and Islamist terrorism, and despite the creation of special squads and units at all levels, the police and government have been at pains to play down the threat posed by armed youth gangs. Far from 'governance through crime', this is governance by trying to persuade the public that crime is far less serious than it actually is.

Ironically, this is also what many mainstream and radical social scientists, offering what they hope will be a comforting sense of perspective to what they believe to be an unreflective and unnecessarily jumpy audience, are doing. But whether, having been patronised and perplexed in this way, the hapless Youth Offending Team (YOT) worker, police officer or social worker who has to live with the reality of gang crime derives any solace from these utterances is doubtful.

Social scientists delivering this shtick almost invariably cite Geoffrey Pearson's magisterial *Hooligan: A History of Respectable Fears* (1984) in support of their arguments. However, to argue, as Pearson does, that detrimental representations of lower-class youth are perpetually recycled by government and the media, is not to argue that every manifestation of youthful crime, violence and disorder has the same origin, meaning or impact.

Whereas some social scientists present contemporary youth crime and disorder as a mere instance of a seemingly timeless, universal, indeed necessary, stage in lower-class adolescent development (Muncie and Hughes 2002; Pitts 2008), a close reading of Pearson's work tells a different story. Pearson's 'hooligans' did not burst unbidden from the pages of history to reassure twenty-first century social scientists that nothing changes. They first came to public attention following an August bank holiday celebration in south-east London in 1898, which culminated in hundreds of arrests for violence, drunkenness and assaults on the police. These young men were well known for terrorising local residents, for their pitched battles, with iron bars, knives, catapults, pistols and revolvers, and for the street robberies that turned many parts of 1890s London into no-go areas.

The 1890s was, of course, the decade that saw the long, disastrous, economic recession that generated the unprecedented poverty, malnutrition, family breakdown, crime, drunkenness and prostitution among working-class children and young people, chronicled by Charles Booth and Beatrice Webb.

The facts contradict the simplistic essentialism of today's 'underdog criminologies'. Rather, *Hooligans* is a warning from history that sustained exposure to acute social and economic disadvantage spawns forms of crime that have catastrophic effects upon the vulnerable populations amongst whom and against whom they are perpetrated.

Change-averse criminologies: the risk factor paradigm

Whereas crime-averse criminologies stress the essential normality of the social deviance enacted by lower-class young people described by 'agents of social control' as 'criminals', the purveyors of the risk factor paradigm are at pains to identify those factors that render young criminals different from the rest of us, and gang members different from them.

Because it is generally believed that even in the most notorious gang neighbourhoods it is only a minority of young people who describe themselves as gang members, some scholars have endeavoured to identify those characteristics, or 'risk factors', that distinguish gang members from their peers. Theirs is a practical endeavour; identifying risk factors in order to fashion interventions that will neutralise them, thereby averting gang membership and ameliorating the gang problem.

Risk factor analysis in the field of youth crime is based on an assessment of the statistical correlates occurring commonly in the lives of young offenders, or drug-users or gang members, whoever the target group happens to be, but much less so in the lives of non-offenders, non-users, non-members, etc. Risk factor analysis does not provide a theory of criminal causation because, as yet, we have been unable to establish which risk factors are causes, which effects and how they interact to produce a criminal act (West and Farrington 1973; Farrington 2002). Because of this, 'risk factors' are less accurate predictors of future offending than is popularly supposed. Indeed, in the seminal *Cambridge Study of Delinquent Development*, which spawned the risk factor paradigm, the researchers found that: 'A majority of the juvenile delinquents, 53 in fact, did not belong to the high-risk group and would not have been predicted' (West and Farrington 1973).

These predictive difficulties are compounded by the fact that almost all of the risk factors said by scholars to predispose young people to gang involvement (see Figure 3.1) tend to be present in the lives of medium to serious, non-gang-involved young offenders, who outnumber gang members by around ten-fold in the USA and fifty-fold in the UK (Thornbury 1998). However, even if a young person clocks up full marks on the risk factor scale, if they live in an area where there are no youth gangs, and this is almost everywhere in the UK, or where gangs are composed of young people of a different ethnic origin, nationality or gender, they cannot become gang members even if they want to. This points to the flawed logic at the heart of the risk factor paradigm which, because it conceives of the gang as a product of the defective attitudes, beliefs and behaviours of its members, cannot account for these complexities.

One might have thought that these limitations would drive the risk factor theorist back to the drawing board, but not so; administrative and strategic imperatives have ensured that the risk factor paradigm has enjoyed an inordinately protracted shelf-life. The reason for its longevity must be sought, however, in its political and administrative utility rather than its explanatory power (Pitts 2007b).

The individualising imperative

The English criminal justice system is predicated upon the eighteenth-century idea that crime is explicable solely in terms of the moral character, proclivities or deficiencies of criminal individuals, and this is reflected in the organisational structures and operational imperatives of the agencies and organisations that service the system. Of course, these police officers, probation officers and Youth Offending Team (YOT) workers recognise that the problem is more complicated than this, but their *raison d'être* is, to use the contemporary argot, 'effective offender management'. And it is to this end that the criminologists and psychologists charged with, and paid for, devising assessment instruments and modes of intervention for these agencies dedicate themselves.

Most contemporary analyses of gang-related risk factors cite six domains: *individual, family, community, school, services and organisations* and *socio-economic policies* (Howell and Egley 2005; and see Figure 3.1), although there is continuing disagreement among politicians and social scientists about which factors at each of these levels, or which of these levels, might be causal and which contingent.

However, in practice, it is usually only the individual and familial risk factors to which criminal justice agencies have the capacity to respond and so they come to occupy the 'foreground'. In consequence, factors associated with *community, school, services and organisations*

Individual
- Prior delinquency
- Illegal gun ownership
- Drug trafficking
- Desire for group rewards such as status, identity, self-esteem, companionship and protection
- Anti-social attitudes
- Aggression
- Alcohol and drug use
- Early or precocious sexual activity
- Violent victimisation

Peer group
- High commitment to delinquent peers
- Street socialisation
- Gang members in class
- Friends who use drugs or who are gang members
- Interaction with delinquent peers
- Pre-teen exposure to stress

School
- Poor school performance
- Low educational aspirations, especially among young females
- Negative labelling by teachers
- High levels of anti-social behaviour
- Few teacher role models
- Educational frustration
- Low attachment to school
- Learning difficulties

Family
- Family disorganisation, including broken homes and parental drug and/or alcohol abuse
- Family violence, neglect and drug addiction
- Family members in a gang
- Lack of adult and parental role models, parental criminality, parents with violent attitudes, siblings with anti-social behaviours
- Extreme economic deprivation

Community
- Social disorganisation, including high poverty and residential mobility
- High crime neighbourhood; neighbourhood youth in trouble
- Presence of gangs in the neighbourhood
- Availability or perceived access to drugs in the neighbourhood
- Availability of firearms
- Cultural norms supporting gang behaviour
- Feeling unsafe in neighbourhood

Figure 3.1 Major risk factors associated with youth gang involvement

and *socio-economic policies* are consigned to the 'background', where they gather dust as the agency continues to plough its individualistic furrow.

Another way of dealing with this mismatch between analysis and capacity is to transform 'background' socio-structural risk factors, or those which flow from inadequate provision, into individual risk factors. This transformation is most obvious in the case of the idea of 'social exclusion', which started life in France as a description of social and economic processes that diminish the life chances of certain social groups, but enters the world of criminal justice as a kind of self-inflicted shortcoming, effected by truancy, joblessness, failure to vote, etc., for which offenders must be encouraged, via the administration of the relevant cognitive-behavioural interventions, to accept responsibility (Pitts 2003, 2007b).

This tendency towards individualisation is particularly evident in the recent development of assessment instruments designed to identify young people at risk of gang involvement. Crime Concern, the crime reduction charity, having undertaken 'extensive, international research' on gang-related risk factors, was, in 2007, developing an assessment tool that could be readily integrated into the existing 'risk-based assessment formats' used by Youth Offending Teams, ASSET and ONSET. But given that the ultimate purpose of these assessment tools is to generate need and risk scores for individuals in order to identify the types of programmes they will be required to pursue, it is highly likely that only individual and familial risk factors will find their way into the mix. Such reductionism is perhaps inevitable when government agencies are handed the responsibility, but lack the capacity, to deal with a complex social, economic and cultural, not simply individual, problem.

Intensity = propensity?

These by no means insignificant difficulties notwithstanding, analytical individualism lives on. Thus, proponents of the risk factor paradigm continue to cite longitudinal studies of young people before, during and after gang membership, which appear to suggest that although both gang members and non-gang members may be exposed to the same risk factors, those who become gang members experience more of them or experience them more intensely (Hill *et al.* 1996). Richard Dukes and colleagues (1997), for example, studied 11,000 US secondary school students, concluding that those with lower self-esteem, lower evaluations of their own academic ability, poorer psychosocial health, and weaker bonds with institutions were more likely to join gangs. However, other research suggests that several of these characteristics are as likely to be a consequence of gang membership as a cause.

Prediction or postdiction

The difficulty of distinguishing causes from consequences is illustrated in the work of Deschenes and Esbensen (1997), who attempted to isolate the risk factors that would predict gang membership by comparing four groups: 'non-delinquents', 'minor delinquents', 'serious delinquents' and 'gang members'. They found that gang members were 'more impulsive', engaged in more 'risk-seeking behavior', were 'less committed to school', and reported less 'communication with, and lower levels of attachment to, their parents'.

However, it is a *sine qua non* that gangs require impulsive, risk-seeking, behaviour; that gang norms dictate that members will be contemptuous of 'authority' in general and school rules in particular, while drug-dealing, and the associated violence, tend to be a preserve of gangs. Moreover, the discovery that one's child has become a violent drug-dealing gangster will, in many families, impede parent–child communication and disrupt emotional attachments.

Gang scholars in the USA have pondered long, hard and somewhat tediously whether young people are recruited into gangs because of their obvious aptitude for crime and violence, whether gang membership facilitates involvement in crime or violence or, indeed, whether it enhances it. The work of Gatti and his colleagues (2005) suggests that the answer is 'yes' to all three.

The American criminologist Terence Thornbury (1998) describes the gang as an escalator, taking 'delinquent' young people to a new and more serious level of criminal involvement. Thus, while the 'delinquent peer group' may act as a vehicle or context for the commission of offences, the severity of which is shaped by the proclivities of individual perpetrators, the gang facilitates the shift to different, and far more serious, levels of crime (Gatti *et al.* 2005; Klein and Maxson 2006).

Indeed, a great deal of research suggests that gang membership has an 'independent effect' upon gang members in several areas. Gang members tend to develop distinctive beliefs and attitudes (Vigil 1987; Sampson and Lauritsen 1994, Kennedy 2007), distinctive behaviours (Short 1997; Pitts 2007b) distinctive mental health problems (Li *et al.* 2002), and distinctive crime patterns (Hagedorn 1998); and they do this, it seems, as a result of their experiences in the gang.

As Jim Short (1997) has observed, most of the factors said to predict gang membership are deduced from what we know about the behaviour of gang members. But if many of these behaviours are a product of gang membership, as much of the research suggests, far from being predictive, they are what Short calls 'postdictive'; inferences about past behaviour derived from events in the present; a case of being unwise after the event.

These uncertainties about the characteristics of gang members arise in large part from the failure of the proponents of the risk factor paradigm to consider the historical conditions that have fostered the emergence of youth gangs and the economic, social and cultural circumstances that have sustained them. It is to these questions that we now turn.

A political economy of the street gang

To gain an understanding of these factors, we must turn to a different type of scholarship: one that also has its roots in North American social science, but repudiates both the functionalist relativism of the youth governance thesis and the abstract empiricism of the risk factor paradigm, and much mainstream North American gang scholarship besides. It employs instead what C. Wright Mills calls the 'sociological imagination', to contextualise the emergence of particular types of youth groupings at particular historical moments (Mills 1959). Studies in this tradition offer what we might call a political economy of the street gang, a perspective that is particularly germane to developments in contemporary Britain.

This shift is necessitated because it was only at the end of the twentieth century, in London, Birmingham and Manchester, that we were confronted with young people who appeared to dress, talk and act like the violent street gangs we had only previously seen on the TV or PlayStation. Because of this, the youth governance thesis, with its insistence on the unknowability of crime, and the risk factor paradigm, which describes a world in which crime never changes, are of limited use to us.

Whereas mainstream 'gang studies' present us with a debased adolescent peer group, awash with 'risk factors' born of poor parenting, bad judgement and a lack of self-control, a political economy of the youth gang views it as a product of, and an actor in, a world demarcated by poverty, sociocultural and racial exclusion, illegitimate opportunity and big city corruption.

The gang as a haven in a heartless world

The systematic study of youth gangs began in the United States in the early part of the twentieth century. These studies, conducted in Chicago by Frederick Thrasher (1929), found that poor, second-generation European migrant youth often formed 'gangs': networks of 'wild', 'unsupervised', adolescents, socialised by the streets rather than by conventional institutions. Thrasher's gangs were involved in crime and plenty of street fighting but they were also the places where their members' emotional and developmental needs were met. Thrasher believed that when societies fail to provide culturally valorised routes into the adult world, lower-class adolescents, via the gang, create their own.

The gang as a political footsoldier

Thrasher, like subsequent gang theorists, emphasises the social isolation of the youth gang; its remoteness from family, community and mainstream social institutions and its conflictual nature (see Decker and Van Winkle 1996; Klein and Maxson 2006). Yet as John Hagedorn (2007) has demonstrated, from the early years of the twentieth century, the youth gangs of Chicago were, in fact, integral to and closely integrated with the violent politics of that city.

Whereas the Chicago migrants of the nineteenth and early twentieth centuries were drawn largely from Europe, the period between the two World Wars saw the Great Migration of African Americans from the Southern States to the industrial cities of the north and Midwest. In the years immediately following World War One, for example, an estimated 450,000 African Americans moved north to Chicago (Valier 2003). This led to the emergence of a racialised urban politics in which the youth gangs, which hung out at the social athletic clubs in the Irish neighbourhoods, were mobilised by the Democratic Party machine not only to prevent black Americans voting but also to ensure that they remained in their neighbourhoods of settlement in Chicago's 'Black Belt'. This created a degree of racial segregation unknown in Britain. John Hagedorn (2007) writes:

In Chicago, social athletic clubs, which were that city's version of New York City's voting gangs, fiercely resisted any penetration of their neighbourhoods by African-Americans. The 1919 race riots were one of the most serious of a rash of racist violence that shook the United States after World War I. The Chicago riots, which killed thirty-eight people, were instigated by white gangs, mainly from the Irish neighbourhoods of Bridgeport and the Back of the Yards, which bordered the so-called Black Belt.

In their biography of Chicago Mayor Richard J. Daley, *American Pharaoh*, Adam Cohen and Elizabeth Taylor (2000) note that:

When Daley was not at school or working, he spent much of his free time at the Hamburg Athletic Club, which met in a nondescript clubhouse at 37th and Emerald, just a few blocks from his home. Hamburg was one of many such clubs in Chicago at the time – others had names like 'Ragen's Colts, 'the Aylwards,' and 'Our Flag' – that were part social circle, part political organization, and part street gang. The athletic clubs placed a premium on toughness and loyalty. The Ragen's Colts' motto could have belonged to any of them: 'Hit me and you hit two thousand.'

The Chicago youth gangs were inextricably involved in the politics of the city, and in *Street Corner Society* (1943) William F. Whyte describes a similar interplay between youth gangs, the political machine and organised crime in Boston's Italian community in the inter-war years. Indeed, Gerald Suttles (1968) argues that in this period the youth gang became a prime mover in the ordered segmentation of urban ethnic communities and hence the political geographies of American cities.

Inevitably, Chicago's African-American young people formed their own gangs in response to white racist violence, a pattern that was repeated later in New York and Los Angeles. In the following decades, white youth gangs across America were involved in violent attacks designed to maintain segregated communities either at the behest or with the tacit support of local political machines.

These studies present the youth gang as an ambiguity. While on the one hand it is a disreputable product of what today we might call social exclusion – detached from, and at odds with, the normal 'socialising institutions' – it is also inextricably bound up with a racial politics bent upon the spatial isolation and disenfranchisement of Black and Hispanic Americans and forms of organised crime that service a prosperous, respectable, clientele. These two elements of gang life were brought together by Richard Cloward and Lloyd Ohlin (1960).

The gang as a collective solution to blocked opportunity

Cloward and Ohlin's *Delinquency and Opportunity* represents the convergence of American structuralism, with its emphasis on the disjunction between universally valorised material goals and aspirations, and access to the institutionalised means for their achievement; and the Chicago School's concern with 'social disorganisation' and the cultural transmission of deviant norms, values and techniques (Park 1929; Park *et al.* 1925; Shaw and McKay 1942; Sutherland and Cressey 1966).

Cloward and Ohlin synthesise these two theoretical traditions in an effort to understand why different types of lower-class New York neighbourhoods produced different types of gangs. The key, they argued, lay in differential access to opportunity, both legitimate and illegitimate, which in turn was determined by differential social organisation. They posited an 'organised' and a 'disorganised' slum. Both are denied access to legitimate opportunity, but organised slums, like the Chicago Irish neighbourhoods described by Thrasher and Hagedorn, are linked into the rackets and maintain mutually beneficial relationships with the police, the political machine and city hall. In short, 'the fix is in'. The 'disorganised slum', by contrast, has no such connections, and so, like the gangs that emerged in Chicago's 'Black Belt' in the 1920s, the only route to status is via demonstrations of physical prowess in gang fights, low-level opportunist street crime and other minor scams, or sport and entertainment (Hagedorn 2007). Reading between the lines of *Delinquency and Opportunity*, it is clear that while the organised slum is inhabited by poor whites, the disorganised slum is home to African and Hispanic Americans who are debarred from both legitimate and illegitimate opportunity. The work of Cloward and Ohlin suggests that to understand the nature of the gang, it is insufficient simply to know the motivations of individuals, or indeed the social and economic conditions that constrain their chances and choices. Rather, it is necessary to understand local cultures and social structures and their fit with the criminal, political and administrative organisations that foster and sustain them. What they also tell us, of course, is that in America race and ethnicity play a crucial role in the allocation of both legitimate and illegitimate opportunity.

Prosperity and the decline of the American street gang

Calculated in US dollars, *Delinquency and Opportunity* was one of the most influential books in human history. On reading it, Bobby Kennedy persuaded his brother John to launch what became the multi-million dollar Kennedy/Johnson Great Society programme (Marris and Rein 1965). Kennedy and Johnson aimed to secure the rights and opportunities previously denied African Americans by circumventing the corrupt political machines in the cities and pumping resources directly into the ghetto. Through affirmative action in education and employment, progressive taxation and income redistribution they hoped to galvanise the indigenous leadership of Cloward and Ohlin's 'disorganised slum', and in doing so transform the urban ghettoes of America.

It was in this period that some youth gangs assumed a political role. John Hagedorn (1997) writes:

> In major U.S. cities, gangs were strongly influenced by revolutionary and civil-rights organizations. The ideologies of groups such as the Black Panther Party, the Brown Berets, and the Young Lords Organization attracted many youths away from the gangs. Many of these political groups in fact began as gangs and aimed their recruiting efforts at the children of the street ... Rivalry between gangs and political groups was balanced by negotiations between them, and gangs joined many movement demonstrations. Gangs also initiated community service agencies, started local businesses, and got federal grants for education and job training. The Conservative Vice Lord Nation, for example, a Chicago gang that came into existence in the 1950s, began multiple social programs and businesses in the 1960s.

The extensively chronicled limitations of the Great Society programme notwithstanding, it is nonetheless the case that in this period large numbers of lower-class Americans were lifted out of poverty. It is also the case that between the late 1950s and the late 1970s the American street gang went into a steep decline. Indeed, *West Side Story*, which premiered on Broadway in 1957, can be seen as marking the end of an era in the history of the American street gang.

Deindustrialisation and the transformation of the American street gang

However, in the 1980s the American street gang returned with a vengeance. This was the decade that saw the collapse of manufacturing industry in the industrial towns of the American Midwest, the 'Rust Belt', soaring structural youth unemployment and unprecedented income polarisation. These economic changes were paralleled by a massive influx of low-priced opiates into the poorest neighbourhoods in the United States (Hagedorn 1998).

In his study of Milwaukee gangs, *People and Folks,* John Hagedorn traces the mutations through which the Milwaukee street gangs passed during this period of seismic social and economic change. The gangs that emerged in the 1960s as a result of the 'bussing' of school students, in an attempt to achieve racial integration, served, Hagedorn argues, primarily as a source of racial and ethnic solidarity and pride, and a base for culturally relevant social activities. Initially, these gangs were principally concerned with style and fashion. There was some inter-group conflict, mainly after dances or at parties, but such enmities were seldom sustained. Members of these groups drank alcohol, smoked marijuana and sometimes engaged in petty crime together. However, the gang was essentially a social group through which successive cohorts of young people passed on their way to adulthood and, as such, the gangs became institutionalised within their communities.

The big change came in the 1980s with the collapse of manufacturing industry and a consequent surge in youth and adult unemployment in the industrial towns of the American Midwest. As the 1980s progressed the Milwaukee gangs came to play a central role in the burgeoning informal economies developing in the poorest neighbourhoods. Thus the teenage gang became a young adult gang, and as it did so it evolved into a 'drug-selling clique of variable organisation' (Hagedorn 1998). Young gang members played a different role in these reconfigured gangs, which came to be dominated by older, drug-selling gang members. Similarly, young women gang members now assumed low-level roles in drug sales, and some were forced into prostitution to sustain their

43

own and other gang members' drug habits. Hagedorn (1998) notes that:

> ... the cocaine economy in these selected parts of three neighbourhoods, at any one time, employed at least 600 people, most of them young male gang members. These young men grossed over $17 million annually, if they individually made their mean of $2,400 per month. We estimate that 1,500 young men were employed in those neighbourhoods alone selling drugs in Milwaukee at some time in the early 1990s. It is likely today that drug sales is the largest single employer of young African American and Latino males in Milwaukee.

The conclusions drawn by Hagedorn about the changing nature of gangs in Milwaukee resonate with the UK experience. In the 1980s, many 'teenage' peer groups in deindustrialised regions like the north-east of England, South Wales, the coalfields of Yorkshire and the Midlands and the west of Scotland became seriously involved in the use and distribution of opiates. As was the case in Milwaukee, opiates filled not only a pressing social and economic need, but an existential one as well.

> Controlled intoxicant use is more likely where a person has other valued life commitments, such as employment, which are incompatible with daily heroin use. One vitally important aspect of unemployment is the devastating impact which it makes upon an individual's time structures ... involving a profound disorientation of daily routines ... The compulsive logic of the heroin lifestyle: get straight – hustle for money – score drugs – get straight and hustle for more money – this effectively solves a major psychological burden of unemployed status. (Pearson 1993)

The scale of the changes described by John Hagedorn was truly remarkable. Whereas in 1975 Walter B. Miller found that six of the twelve largest US cities had a major gang problem, research undertaken in the early 1990s by Irving Spergel and David Curry (1993) revealed that the problem had now spread to ten of the twelve major cities. Moreover, Spergel and Curry found increases in gang activity in cities of all sizes, with a remarkable 63 per cent increase in the far smaller 'new gang cities'. By the mid 1990s, chapters of what had originally been the Los Angeles-based 'Crips' and 'Bloods' could be found in 45 other cities, mainly in the Midwest and the West. And in all of these cities it was 'minority' and migrant youth who were most heavily involved.

Ethnicity and gang affiliation

While most official accounts of the 'gang problem' are at pains to obscure its racial dimension, the youth gangs that emerged in 1980s America were overwhelmingly Black and Hispanic. In the USA, as in Europe, it was non-white, non-indigenous and migrant youth who were the major casualties of deindustrialisation. A study undertaken by Mercer Sullivan in the 1980s points up the role of ethnicity in gang affiliation. Building on the work of Cloward and Ohlin, in *Getting Paid* (1989) Sullivan tracked three groups of lower-class adolescents from the Bronx – Hispanic, African and white Americans – through their adolescent years. Whereas at 14 and 15 they were all involved in similar kinds of legal and illegal activity, by their late teens most of the white youngsters had been absorbed into reasonably paid, unionised, skilled and semi-skilled industrial work that was effectively unavailable to non-white applicants. The Hispanic young people ended up either in short-term, low-paid work, on 'dead-end' training schemes, unemployed or working in illicit 'chop shops', recycling stolen car parts. By their late teens, some of the African American young people were able to take advantage of the remaining vestiges of the Kennedy/Johnson 'affirmative action' programmes, to enter lower-level public service jobs. Others, however, were drawn into the local crack-dealing street gangs that offered high rewards for high risks. What Sullivan shows is that opportunity, both legal and illegal, is crucially demarcated by social class, ethnicity and a racialised politics that grants legitimate opportunity to some but not others. But the pluralistic world that Sullivan depicts was soon to be swept away by the 'secession of the successful' and 'hyper-ghettoisation'.

The collapse of the ghetto

Because of the blatantly institutionalised and at times violent racism chronicled by Cloward and Ohlin (1960), Sullivan (1989) and Hagedorn (2007), black people in twentieth-century urban America were compelled to develop their own social worlds. These 'ghettos' were to a considerable extent socially self-sufficient, held together by the twin pillars of the church and the black business community.

> The organizations that formed the framework of everyday life for urban blacks were created and run by African Americans. The black press, churches, lodges and fraternal orders, social clubs and political machine knit together a dense fabric of resources and sociability that supported African American ethnic pride and group uplift. For their 200,000 members, the five hundred religious congregations that dotted the South Side were not only places of worship and entertainment but also a potent vehicle for individual and collective mobility. In the economic realm, too, African Americans could seek or sustain the illusion of autonomy and advancement. To be sure, Negro enterprise was small-scale and commercially weak: the three most numerous types of black-owned firms were beauty parlors, grocery stores, and barber shops. But the popular 'doctrine of the "Double-Duty Dollar," ' according to which buying from black concerns would 'advance the race,' promised a path to economic independence from whites. And the 'numbers game,' with some 500 stations employing 5,000 and paying yearly wages in excess of a million dollars for three daily drawings, seemed to prove that one could indeed erect a self-sustaining economy within Black Metropolis. (Wacquant 2004)

However, in the 1980s, deindustrialisation and widespread unemployment precipitated the secession of the successful, as those local businesses that had not gone under moved out to more propitious locations; to be followed by the last vestiges of the economically active black workforce and a socially mobile black intelligentsia (Wilson 1987). Meanwhile, swingeing cuts in public services and welfare benefits meant that the predicament of those left behind worsened dramatically. Loïc Wacquant (2004) describes this as the 'collapse of the ghetto'; a process in which simultaneous upward and downward mobility in the black community opens up social and economic opportunity for some as it attenuates it for others.

The concurrent loss of influential social networks fostered by the church and the black business community serves to fracture pre-existing political and racial solidarity and the political power that some 'ghetto' communities were able to exert in North American cities. This 'collapse of the ghetto' is followed, Wacquant argues, by a process of 'hyper-ghettoisation' in which material deprivation, the absence of regulating 'social relations' and the violence associated with the burgeoning drugs trade leads to an intensification of 'black on black' violence.

> By the 1980s, the basic institutions on Chicago's South Side were (i) astringent and humiliating welfare programs, bolstered and replaced by 'workfare' after 1996, which restricted access to the public aid rolls and pushed recipients into the low-wage labor market; (ii) decrepit public housing that subjected its tenants and the surrounding population to extraordinary levels of criminal insecurity, infrastructural blight, and official scorn; (iii) failing institutions of public health and education operating with resources, standards, and results typical of Third World countries; and (iv) not least, the police, the courts, probation officers, parole agents, and 'snitches' recruited by the thousands to extend the mesh of state surveillance and capture deep into the hyperghetto. (Wacquant 2004)

In the process, we see a massive hike in African-American imprisonment rates, exceeding those of the Soviet Union at the height of Stalin's purges and South Africa when the anti-apartheid struggle was at its most intense. Indeed, in the last half century, the ethnic composition of US prisons has shifted from 70 per cent white to 70 per cent black and Latino. These developments, Wacquant argues, create a 'deadly symbiosis' a kind of cultural cross-pollination in which the ghetto is prisonised and the prison is ghettoised.

The colonial legacy

Paradoxically, these prisonised neighbourhoods are, at once, places where the 'unsuccessful' lie immobilised at the bottom of the social structure and a destination for newcomers, hoping to better themselves (Sassen 2007). But as Thrasher and his colleagues at the University of Chicago discovered a century ago, many will simply be swapping one form of oppression for another. Philippe Bourgois (1995) writes:

> For those who emigrated from the island [Puerto Rico], culture shock has obviously been more profound. Literally overnight, the new immigrants whose rural-based cultural orientation and self-esteem was constructed around interpersonal webs of *respeto* [respect] organised around complex categories of age,

gender, and kinship found themselves transformed into 'racially' inferior pariahs. Ever since their arrival in the United States they have been despised and humiliated with a virulence that is specific to North America's history of polarised race relations and ethnically segmented immigrant labour markets.

In his study of Puerto Rican crack-dealers in the East Harlem barrio, Bourgois (1995) describes how, confronted by almost insuperable blocks to legitimate opportunity and institutionalised racism, crack- dealing, with its associated violence, offers them a place, albeit an immensely dangerous one, where some respect can be reclaimed.

Similarly, in *Born Fi Dead* (2003) Laurie Gunst chronicles the lives of members of the Jamaican posses that came to dominate the US crack business in the 1990s. Condemned to abject poverty in the shanty towns of Kingston, these young men embraced an alternative world constructed of wild fantasy and brute reality in equal measure:

> These island desperados are the bastard offspring of Jamaica's violent political 'shitstem' (as the Rastafarians long ago dubbed it) and the gun-slinger ethos of American movies.

Like Bourgois' Puerto Rican crack-dealers, their family relationships are continually undermined by poverty and economic migration, while political violence, police brutality and ghetto shoot-outs produce a kind of compulsive, misogynistic, but strangely detached, masculinity. Gunst is asking Conroy about the difference between killing in the movies and real killing:

> To an outsider it might look like 'Damn, these guys are mean!' But being from Jamaica, you see it growing up, you see it all your life. Even before I killed somebody, I felt like I killed before. I think maybe Hollywood had a part in the rude-boy thing, with the movies they put out like certain westerns. Jamaicans act out a lot of that stuff, want to be tough like outlaws. Even Delroy. Every time he would shoot somebody, we would say, 'Hey! You just got another notch on your gun.'

Reading Bourgois and Gunst, it is clear that these modes of physical and psychological survival do not simply fall away because the subject relocates to another country, particularly if their social and political marginality at home is echoed, and reproduced, in the impoverished neighbourhoods to which they migrate.

The prospects for change

John Hagedorn (2007) is pessimistic about the prospects for change in the USA, pointing to the centrality of the 'war on drugs' and the apparently inexorable expansion of the criminal justice apparatus as part and parcel of this endeavour. He presents a world in which people excluded from the 'information economy' are increasingly forced to the margins of the economic, social and cultural mainstream, to do the best they can with such resources as they have. This, he argues, must inevitably result in a growth in crime.

> Unwired poor communities began to resemble areas of the Third World, with a burgeoning informal economy taking the place of lost legal jobs. This informal neighbourhood economy includes off-the-books enterprises, like street-side car repair, hair styling, house-painting, child care, and street vending, as well as a host of illegal activities. And the most profitable informal enterprise is the business of drugs. Poor neighbourhoods, as Castells points out, are becoming the shop floor of the international drug economy.

In the late 1990s these towns were attempting to develop new 'information-based' economies. However, as Hagedorn observes, in Columbus, Ohio, for example, where unemployment was falling and median incomes were rising, a quarter of the black population in Ohio's Franklin county lived under the poverty line compared with a local average of a little over 10 per cent. This impoverishment of the black community has been paralleled by severe cutbacks in 'human service' expenditure, which has deepened the problems occasioned by economic decline. The predicament of black residents has been compounded by growing income inequality and the acute status-frustration it engenders in a culture that places a high value upon material success. Hagedorn also notes that 'post-industrial economic growth is notoriously uneven' and that the very forces that are bringing some middle-income earners back to the centre of economic life are propelling others to the margins:

49

... to many observers, economic segmentation is creating an underclass of mainly urban blacks and Hispanics who are not sharing in the benefits of economic expansion. Coinciding with this economic transformation, we are witnessing a rebirth of youth gangs in many small and medium sized cities and their entrenchment in larger cities. (Hagedorn 1998)

For much of the twentieth century, Americans who have thought deeply about youthful crime and disorder have focused upon questions of change, assimilation and exclusion. They have asked why the 'melting pot' has produced such deep racial and social divisions and why, for so many of America's poorest young people, the 'American Dream' has become a nightmare.

British youth studies

If North American gang studies emphasise the role of race and social exclusion in the formation of youth gangs, for British youth studies social class is the great arbiter of destiny. Indeed, until the mid 1960s there were hardly any British studies of lower-class youth crime *per se* and even those that touched upon the subject were primarily concerned with working-class culture (Jephcott 1954; Mays 1954; Willmott 1966). T.R. Fyvel's *The Insecure Offenders* (1969), marks a departure from this tradition, offering a social-psychological profile of the Teddy boys, but it was David Downes' study of working-class young offenders in east London, *The Delinquent Solution* (1966), that established the link between British and North American scholarship. Utilising theoretical categories devised within the American sociological tradition, Downes endeavoured to determine whether or not US-style youth gangs, existed in the UK. He didn't find any gangs but he did find what Sennett and Cobb (1972) have called 'the hidden injuries of class'.

Downes' study eloquently portrays the pains of incorporation into the lower echelons of an inequitable class system. Far from the rebellion triggered by social and economic exclusion evidenced in the exploits of American street gangs, in *The Delinquent Solution* Downes finds only a rueful resignation.

Yet the working-class boy who has undergone this process, who has been hampered in school by his attachment to working class values, reacts to 'failure' not by frustration, reaction-formation etc., but by the reaffirmation of the working class value-system. Its social constraints still broadly apply, and the normative early marriage – with its family responsibilities, need for a steady job, need to 'get by' if not 'get on' – rob the leisure context of its attraction: alternative solutions have been provided. The need for 'exploit' is killed. (1966: 258)

However, a decade later this 'working class value-system' was under threat. By the mid 1970s it was clear that the post-war boom was faltering, that youth unemployment was rising sharply, and that growing numbers of young people were falling out of the working class into a sociocultural limbo.

It was the Birmingham Centre for Contemporary Cultural Studies (BCCCS) that chronicled how these young people, through their flamboyant, ritualised, subcultural styles, attempted to resist the changes being thrust upon them. Thus for John Clarke (1975) 'skinhead' is a response to the fragmentation of white working-class community; an attempt to 'magically recover' a partially imagined, disappearing working-class world. Skinheads did this, he argued, through the caricatured enactment of what they took to be core working-class values, in highly visible displays of defensive territoriality and an unremitting hostility to newcomers, enacted in those working-class neighbourhoods whose racial and class constitution was undergoing a dramatic transformation and, even more spectacularly, on the football terraces.

In the late 1970s race and racial oppression became a major focus of the work of the BCCCS, and in *Policing the Crisis* (1978) Stuart Hall and his associates, drawing upon Stanley Cohen's seminal *Folk Devils and Moral Panics*, charted the governmental and media orchestration of the 1980s 'mugging panic' and the consequent demonisation of black youth.

Racial oppression was also the focus of Ken Pryce's remarkable *Endless Pressure* (1979), an ethnographic study chronicling the struggles of the African Caribbean residents of the St Paul's district of Bristol as they cope with low incomes, sub-standard housing, separation from loved ones and racial antagonism. Like Gunst's *Born Fi Dead* and Hagedorn's *People and Folks*, Pryce's *Endless Pressure* describes how, confronted with blocks to legitimate opportunity, young people may adopt strategies that, while being ultimately self-defeating, allow them to retain a sense of self-respect. But *Endless Pressure* is also a tribute to the creativity of oppressed peoples, the diverse adaptations they are able to develop and the powerful role of culture, religion and social class in determining what these are.

The intensification of policing in areas of African Caribbean settlement at the start of the 1980s culminated in the 1981 'riots' in Brixton and other towns and cities throughout England and Wales. While some commentators, like Paul Gilroy in *The Empire Strikes Back* (1992), celebrated the riots and black youth crime as resistance to state-sponsored racial oppression, others, like John Lea and Jock Young (1988), argued that, given the high level of intra-racial crime and violence in these neighbourhoods far from being an expression of resistance, such crime simply compounded the victim's oppression. In such a situation, they said, radical criminologists could not, in any straightforward way, be 'on the side' of the socially disadvantaged perpetrators since to indulge in such unreflective partisanship was to ignore the plight of the victimised black community.

In the same way that by the end of the 1980s some areas of African-Caribbean settlement in London, Liverpool, Birmingham and Manchester had become effectively detached from the economic and sociocultural mainstream, so had many parts of other British provincial cities and out-of-town housing estates. And it was to one of these 'forgotten places', the Meadowell estate in Newcastle Upon Tyne, that Beatrix Campbell returned in the wake of the 1991 riots. In *Goliath: Britain's Dangerous Places* (1993) she writes:

> Crime was part of the economy, and a part of what it put up with. Every one of the children at one of the estate's primary schools depended on clothing grants and three quarters depended on free school meals. A quarter of the young men up to the age of 24 were unemployed and long-term unemployment amongst males was the highest in the North East ... In the period between the Sixties and the Nineties the region lost most of its staple jobs for men in the shipyards. In the year before the [1991 1992 and 1993] riots, it had the highest crime rate in the country.

There are resonances here of Hagedorn's *People and Folks* (1998).

Indeed, recent work in youth studies comes even closer to the US tradition, largely because in twenty-first century Britain the phenomena they study bear a closer resemblance to US youth crime. *Youth Crime and Youth Culture in the Inner City* by Bill Sanders (2005), an American working in Britain, for example, is a study of black and mixed heritage young people involved in street robbery and drug dealing in south London. Despite the fact that some of these young people come from lower middle-class homes, with parents who are white-collar workers or para-professionals in public services, the power of local street cultures means that once involved, their criminal careers escalate. Similarly, Simon Hallsworth's *Street Crime* (2005) emphasises the powerful role of street cultures in sustaining street robbery.

In the next chapter we consider whether, and to what extent we are witnessing the convergence of North American and British modes of youth crime, but in doing so we endeavour to abide by C. Wright Mills' injunction to 'grasp history and biography and the relations between the two within society' in order to produce a political economy of youth gangs in Britain (Mills 1959).

Chapter 4

Why here? Why now?

This town, is coming like a ghost town
Why must the youth fight against themselves?
Government leaving the youth on the shelf
This place, is coming like a ghost town
No job to be found in this country
Can't go on no more
The people getting angry

The Specials, 'Ghost Town' (1981)

Today industrial labour – or what is left of it – is very much within the majority class of those who have an interest in preserving the status quo. The underclass on the contrary is a mere category, a victim. It is unlikely to organise and defend the many similar yet not really common interests of its members. They are, if the cruelty of the statement is pardonable, not needed. The rest could and would quite like to live without them.

Ralph Dahrendorf (1994)

Throughout the post-war period the USA has been a shaping influence upon the economy, culture and politics of the UK and this has fostered the erroneous belief that what happens in the United States today is destined to happen in the UK tomorrow. The late 1950s saw an upsurge of gang violence in the USA, most memorably depicted in the musical *West Side Story*, raising fears in the UK that we too could be facing teenage gang warfare on our city streets before too long.

But, in the same way that Cliff Richard was no Elvis Presley, the scuffles between Teddy boys outside the Streatham Locarno on a Saturday night were at best a pale shadow of the action on the Lower East Side.

The absence, until recently, of 'American-style' armed youth gangs in the UK is probably attributable to a mixture of social, economic and cultural factors. It is widely accepted that the USA has traditionally been prepared to tolerate a greater degree of poverty and social inequality than has been the case in the UK or mainland Europe (Wilson 1987). Whereas until the 1950s the UK was, to all intents and purposes, a mono-racial society, the USA is a country constituted from successive waves of poor migrants. In the nineteenth century these migrants came from Europe, but the 'Great Migration', between the two World Wars, saw huge numbers of African Americans moving to the industrial cities of the north and Midwest. As we have seen, this led to levels of spatial segregation by race unknown in Britain, and the emergence of a violent, racialised, urban politics. Unsurprisingly, therefore, the conflict generated by the tolerance of poverty in the USA has often taken the form of inter-racial violence between poor young people of different ethnic origins living in adjacent neighbourhoods.

Through most of the post-war period in Britain, the traditional society *par excellence,* a well-developed welfare state, redistributive taxation and a public housing strategy that promoted greater demo-graphic and social heterogeneity than in the USA, has tended to act as a bulwark against economic, racial and class 'ghettoisation' (Pitts 2003).

In the UK, social status has traditionally been ascribed on the basis of social class and this has served to obscure and to some extent legitimise the inequitable distribution of wealth and opportunity. As a result, material aspirations have been bounded by social class aspirations, and this has served to reduce the status frustration of those social groups prevented from achieving the 'glittering prizes'. Messner and Rosenfeld (1994) have argued that in the USA, the apotheosis of the non-traditional, deregulated, 'open' society, material success is the key determinant of social status, and no cultural ceiling is placed upon material aspirations. As a result, when lower-class Americans encounter structural blocks to legitimate opportunity they are likely to experience heightened status frustration, blame the system rather than themselves and devise collective, illegitimate, solutions to this problem (Cloward and Ohlin 1960; Sullivan 1989).

55

If this is so, then we can see that the youth gang might provide an ideal vehicle for such a collective endeavour.

Widespread opiate use hit the USA earlier and harder than the UK. Since the mid 1970s, opiate-dealing has become a core activity, indeed the *raison d'être*, for many US youth gangs (Hagedorn 1998), and the remarkable expansion of the gang phenomenon in the USA in the 1980s paralleled and was facilitated by the rapid spread of illicit drug use. When linked with a strong cultural tradition of gun ownership, self-defence and self-reliance, as evidenced by popular portrayals of violence in general and guns in particular as problem-solving devices within US culture (Young 1999), this combination becomes lethal. Indeed, it appears that the 40 per cent increase in youth homicides in the USA in the 1970s and, more particularly, the 200 per cent increase in youth gang killings, was a product of the US youth gang emerging as the 'shop floor of the international drug economy' (Castells 2000, cited in Hagedorn 1998).

For most of the post-war period, youth crime in the UK has been a pale reflection of youth crime in the USA. There was simply much more of it there and it was both far more serious and far more violent. However, the past two decades in the UK have witnessed seismic economic and political changes that have eroded many of the differences between the two societies.

The great reversal

A major effect of the attempt to introduce US-style economic liberalism into the UK was the reversal, from 1979 onwards, of the post-war tendency towards a narrowing of the gap between rich and poor and the growth of both absolute and relative deprivation. Between 1981 and 1991 the number of workers earning half the national average wage or less, the Council of Europe poverty line, rose from 900,000 to 2.4 million. In the same period those earning over twice the national average rose from 1.8 to 3.1 million. In February 1999, the gap between the gross domestic product (GDP) of the poorest and the richest regions in the UK was the widest in the European Union (EU). The richest region, Inner London, ranked against an EU average of 100, scored 222. The poorest regions, like Merseyside and West Wales, scored less than 75, rendering them eligible for EU 'special aid' (Pitts 2003).

The rolling back of the state

In the heyday of the welfare state, UK governments endeavoured to ameliorate the depredations of the capitalist market by direct intervention in the social and economic spheres. With the advent of neo-liberalism in the late 1970s this began to change; a change that culminated in New Labour's politics of the Third Way in the early 1990s (Giddens, 1999).

In what Fawcett *et al.* (2004) have called the new Social Investment State, rather than protecting the citizen from the vagaries of the capitalist market, the role of the state is to facilitate their integration into the market via the provision of Welfare to Work programmes on the one hand and reductions in state benefits on the other. As a result, Bill Jordan (2004) argues, 'Society has become an association for people who shouldn't need to associate or a club in which members tell each other to pull themselves together.'

David Garland (2001) observes that the advent of the politics of the Third Way marks the demise of the 'solidarity project'. In this new politics, earlier social democratic accounts of the relationship between the individual and society and the citizen and the state are inverted, with the responsibilities of the state to its citizens de-emphasised in favour of the duties owed by citizens to the state.

Thus, Pierre Bourdieu (1998) argues, the 'left hand of the state', which once assumed responsibility for creating the social, educational and economic conditions for effective citizenship, is stilled, while the 'right hand of the state', which acts to impose order and discipline and contain or expel those unable to meet their civic and economic obligations, is given free rein. Zygmunt Bauman (2004) states the matter succinctly:

> 'Welfare state' institutions are being progressively dismantled and phased out, while restraints previously imposed on business activities and on the free play of market competition and its consequences are removed. The protective functions of the state are being tapered to embrace a small minority of the unemployable and the invalid, though even this minority tends to be re-classified from the issue of social care into the issue of law and order: an incapacity to participate in the market game tends to be increasingly criminalized.

Nowhere was the impact of these changes more evident than in the housing market.

A concentration of disadvantage

The gangs we studied in the *Red*, *White* and *Blue* boroughs had their homes in what in the 1980s came to be known as 'social housing' estates. In 1979 almost half of Britain's population lived in council housing. A generation later, only 12 per cent were housed by the local authority, with another 6 per cent living in flats and houses owned and managed by housing associations and co-operatives. The introduction of market mechanisms into the public sector housing via Margaret Thatcher's 'right to buy' and 'tenant incentive' schemes had the effect of diminishing the amount of available housing while shifting more affluent tenants into the private sector (Page 1993). By 1982, sales of council homes to former tenants had reached 200,000 a year. Between 1970 and 1990, owner-occupation in the UK rose from 55.3 per cent to 67.6 per cent of households. This 'secession of the successful' meant that increasingly it was the least 'successful' who were entering social housing. As Andrew Adonis and Stephen Pollard wrote in 1998:

> Twenty years ago, if you wanted to find a poor family, you had to ring a number of door bells of typical council flats before you found one. Today, arrive at a council estate, ring any bell, and you have probably found one ... no one chooses to live in a council house – especially if they want to get on.

And as Malcolm Dean (1997) observes:

> This happened despite the warnings of housing professionals about the problems which public housing projects generated when they were confined to the poor, the unemployed and elderly.

As predicted, as the 1980s progressed relatively prosperous, middle-aged, higher-income families left social housing, to be replaced by poorer, younger, often lone-parent families (Page 1993). Between 1984 and 1994 annual residential mobility in social housing increased from 4 per cent to 7 per cent of households. Whereas in the 1980s and 1990s 40 per cent of heads of households in social housing were aged 65 or over, 75 per cent of newly formed households entering social housing were headed by someone aged between 16 and 29. A high proportion of these new residents were unemployed, not least because they included a heavy concentration of lone parents. As Dean (1997) noted:

Two quite distinct communities are emerging within the sector with quite profound differences in lifestyles and culture. At one end there are the established elderly residents, who have lived in social housing all their lives and who remember a time when having a council home was a desirable goal. At the other end are the new, younger residents, frequently suffering from multiple problems: unemployment, poverty, poor work skills and perhaps mental illness and drug abuse as well.

In its report *Bringing Britain Together*, the government's Social Exclusion Unit (1998) identified 1,370 housing estates in Britain which it characterised as 'poor neighbourhoods which have poverty, unemployment, and poor health in common, and crime usually comes high on any list of residents' concerns'.

Family poverty

At the beginning of the 1980s the average household income of council house residents was 73 per cent of the national average. At the beginning of the 1990s this had fallen to 48 per cent. According to the Joseph Rowntree Foundation, by 1995 over 50 per cent of council households had no breadwinner and 95 per cent qualified for some form of means-tested benefit (Income Support, Jobseekers' Allowance, Family Credit and Disability Working Allowance). By 1997, 25 per cent of children and young people in Britain were living in these neighbourhoods.

Most of the young people in our study had grown up in poverty. Their neighbourhoods are among the most socially disadvantaged in England and Wales. In 2004, 45,905 of Red borough's 222,340, residents (20 per cent) were deemed to be 'income deprived', while 61 of Red borough's 145 'super output areas' (SOAs, neighbourhoods of around 1,500 people) are among the most deprived 20 per cent in England and Wales, and 23 are in the top 5 per cent. Unsurprisingly, most of these SOAs have high rates of street crime, drug-dealing and firearms offences and are home to Red borough's youth gangs.

Over 40 per cent of White borough's children live on or near the poverty line. In 2001, in the wards where gang activity is most prevalent, between 47 per cent and 60 per cent of them lived in families eligible for means-tested benefits. The poorest ward in the borough is the stamping ground of its largest and most violent gang.

In a national survey, the White borough ward with the second highest number of offending young people in 2006, was ranked 431st out of the 8,414 wards in England for child poverty, with an index score of 60.0; against 88.7 for Wirral (the highest) and 0.5 for Gerrards Cross North (the lowest).

Eligibility for free school meals is often used as a proxy indicator of poverty. In 2002 38 per cent of White borough's children were eligible for free school meals, against a national average of 17 per cent. In the ward with the highest level of street robberies, where White borough's most violent gangs are located, eligibility for free school meals was 52 per cent.

Structural youth unemployment

During the 1980s Britain lost 20 per cent of its industrial base. In Sheffield, for example, a city of 200,000 people, between 1979 and 1989 40,000 jobs were lost. Between 1984 and 1997, the numbers of young people aged 16–24 in the labour market shrank by almost 40 per cent (Coleman 1999). Some were absorbed into the government's Welfare to Work programmes and others gravitated towards higher education, but a substantial proportion can now be found in the unemployment figures.

These changes have had a particularly detrimental effect upon black and minority ethnic young people aged 16 to 24, and on young men in particular, who are substantially more likely than their white counterparts to be unemployed – 36 per cent of black Caribbeans, 31 per cent of Pakistanis and Bangladeshis, 26 per cent of Indians and 14 per cent of Whites (Office of National Statistics 1998).

Non-employment (unemployment and 'invalidity') in Red borough is high, and as with White and Blue boroughs it is particularly high for people described as 'Black/British' and 'Mixed'. Table 4.1 gives non-employment rates by race for those of working age in Red borough. While it reveals high rates of non-employment for Mixed and Black/British residents in the borough for all age groups, it understates youth non-employment rates in gang-affected communities, which are significantly higher, topping 60 per cent on some estates.

Saskia Sassen (2007) sees falling incomes and youth and ethnic minority unemployment as indicative of longer-term changes in urban 'employment regimes' that have, she argues, destroyed the 'bridge' from low-wage jobs and poverty into sustainable working class or middle class employment:

Table 4.1 Non-employment by ethnicity as a percentage of working age population, 2004

	Male	Female
White	5.3	2.7
Mixed	14.8	15.3
Black/British	20.3	30.3

Source: Red Borough Economic Profile Update, 2005

It is the downgrading of manufacturing that has played a crucial role in cutting off the bridges that used to enable low-income youth to move into reasonably paying jobs in a world of expanding, mostly unionised factories. Now many of these jobs are gone or have been downgraded to sweatshop work, often drawing on immigrant workers. This cuts off one of the key ways for youth to mainstream themselves out of gang life. The result has been that gang members stay longer in gangs and are more likely to participate in the criminal economy ...

These [jobs] are not attractive options for young people who, even when poor, are raised in ideological contexts that emphasise success, wealth, career. Politically and theoretically this points to an employment context that can create both a growing demand for immigrant labour and the alienation of native workers. (2007: 104, 106)

Young, black and estranged

In contrast with the steady upward educational, occupational and social mobility of a substantial section of Britain's black and Asian citizens, in the slump that began in the late 1980s many other black and Asian Britons experienced downward mobility, finding themselves immobilised at the bottom of the social and economic structure. By 1995, 40 per cent of African Caribbeans and 59 per cent of Pakistanis and Bangladeshis in the UK were located in the poorest fifth of the population. This contrasts with only 18 per cent of the white population (Joseph Rowntree Foundation 1995). In London by the mid 1990s, up to 70 per cent of residents on the poorest housing estates were from ethnic minorities (Power and Tunstall 1995; Robins 1992; Palmer and Pitts 2006). Lynsey Hanley (2007) writes:

> You can take this social stratification further, by looking at the height of the council property they rent: if they live above the fifth floor of a local authority block in England they are more likely not only to be working class, but also to be from an ethnic minority ... The effect of this spreading-out of wealth through private ownership rather than state-led redistribution, however, has been to make the poor suffer most, and to perpetuate a situation in which the worst off are also the worst housed.

The neighbourhood effect

The Pittsburgh Youth Study analysed the lives of over 15,000 young people in the city (Wikstrom and Loeber 1997). The researchers found that offending by subjects with no, or very low, individual and familial risk factors occurred significantly more frequently in the lowest socio-economic status (SES) neighbourhoods, and that the relation between these risk factors and serious offending 'breaks down' for those living in the most disadvantaged communities. These findings challenge what Elliott Currie (1985) calls the 'fallacy of autonomy', the idea that the behaviour of individuals and their families can be separated out from the circumstances in which they live. Malcolm Gladwell (2000) states the matter succinctly when he says that given the choice it is far better to come from a troubled family in a good neighbourhood than a good family in a troubled neighbourhood.

Economic segregation

Some commentators argue that the spatial concentration of social disadvantage is a result of poor neighbourhoods becoming segregated from local economies (see McGahey 1986, for example). Economic segregation sets in train processes that further isolate these neighbourhoods because, as McGahey (1986) suggests, residents in poor, high-crime neighbourhoods tend to derive their livelihoods from the 'informal economy' and 'secondary sector' labour markets, characterised by low wages and sporadic, dead-end work, supplemented by 'government transfers, employment and training programmes, crime and illegal hustles' which 'constitute important additional sources of income, social organisation and identity for the urban poor'.

Another key characteristic of high-crime neighbourhoods, and this was the case in the Red, White and Blue boroughs, is that skilled, economically mobile adult workers leave them, and their departure serves to further destabilise the neighbourhood, thereby deepening family poverty. McGahey (1986) writes:

> The quality and quantity of jobs in a neighbourhood determine the ways people form households, regulate their own, and the public behaviour of others, and use public services. The resulting neighbourhood atmosphere then helps to shape the incentives for residents to engage in legitimate employment or income-oriented crime. A high level of adult involvement in primary sector employment spawns stable households, stable families, stable social relationships and enhanced vocational opportunities for the next generation.

And, of course, a low level of adult involvement in primary sector employment produces the opposite.

Socio-political marginalisation

A further characteristic of these neighbourhoods is that residents tend not to be connected to locally influential social and political networks (Wilson 1987). This denies them information about social, educational or vocational opportunity as well as access to the political influence that could improve their situation (Morris 1995).

It is not that people in these neighbourhoods have no 'social capital' but rather that their social capital tends to be 'sustaining but constraining', enabling them to 'get by', to survive the day-to-day struggle, but not to 'get on', by moving out of their present situation and into the social and economic mainstream (De Souza Briggs 1998; Pettit and McLanahan 2001).

Discreditation and stigma

Moreover, living in a poor neighbourhood, among what Detleif Baum (1996) has described as a 'discredited population', makes residents the object of stigma and discrimination, which can undermine their self-esteem, making them even less willing to move beyond the confines of the neighbourhood.

> Young people sense this discreditation in their own environment, in school or in the cultural or leisure establishments. Through this they experience stigmatisation of their difference, of their actions, and the perceived incompetence of the people they live among. The options for action are limited and possibilities for gaining status-enhancing resources are made more difficult. At some stage the process becomes a self-fulfilling prophecy; young people and adults come to think that there must be 'something in it' when their characteristics and ways of behaving are stigmatised, and some become confirmed in this uncertainty. (Baum 1996)

Surveys have repeatedly shown that people who live in poor areas tend to condemn petty crime and benefit fraud (Dean and Taylor-Gooby 1992). However, the struggles of everyday life in a poor neighbourhood can mean that they find it difficult to live up to these values (Wilson 1987). They may therefore 'go along with' and in some cases benefit from the criminality in the neighbourhood. This, in turn, contributes to the stigma that attaches to them and thereby compounds their isolation. Beyond this, it also gives out an ambiguous message to young people who are involved in or may be on the threshold of crime (Kennedy 2007).

Alternative cognitive landscapes

In the 1980s and 1990s the situation of the poorest segment of Britain's black and minority ethnic (BME) community worsened significantly (Palmer and Pitts 2006). For some, the effects of structural youth and adult unemployment and family poverty were exacerbated by negative experiences in school and confrontations with the police on the street. As a result, many people in the black community made a link between their present situation and the racial oppression experienced by their forebears (Pryce 1979). Their sense of being 'stuck' was compounded by the departure of the upwardly mobile, politically articulate sections of the black community (Wilson 1987; Palmer and Pitts 2006). To be socially excluded with the prospect of eventual inclusion may generate hope, but as the 1990s progressed, the situation of these black citizens, marooned on the social margins, appeared to be growing steadily worse (Power and Tunstall 1995). Ben Bowling and Coretta Phillips (2006) argue that such undeserved injustice generates frustration and rage, while David Kennedy (2007) maintains that it also promotes 'norms and narratives supportive of gang violence'. James Short (1997) argues that over time these norms and narratives foster 'alternative cognitive landscapes':

> Mutual suspicion and concern with respect pervade the ghetto poor community. Under such circumstances social order becomes precarious ... Out of concern for being disrespected, respect is easily violated. Because status problems are mixed with extreme resource limitations, people – especially young people – exaggerate the importance of symbols, often with life-threatening consequences ... These consequences are exacerbated by the widespread belief that authorities view black life as cheap, hardly worth their attention. This view is reinforced when black-on-white crime receives more attention by authorities and by the media than does black-on-black crime. The result is that people feel thrown back on their own limited resources. They arm, take offence, and resist in ways that contribute to the cycle of violence.

In these circumstances, Short argues, wider cultural values become unviable and these young people come to occupy a far bleaker, 'alternative cognitive landscape', developing what is sometimes called a 'soldier mentality', characterised by a heightened sensitivity to threat and a constant preparedness for action (Sampson and Lauritson 1994). And this, as Decker and Van Winkle (1996) have demonstrated, tends to isolate gang members from the social and cultural mainstream to the extent that, eventually, they may only feel at ease in the gang.

Chapter 5

From a blag to a business

Al Capone's guns don't argue.

Praice Buster (1964)

The redistribution of crime and victimisation

As we have seen, throughout the 1980s and 1990s in Britain, those people most vulnerable to criminal victimisation and those most likely to victimise them were progressively thrown together on the poorest housing estates. As a result, although crime has been dropping steadily in the UK since 1992, crime in areas of acute social deprivation has, in many cases, become far more serious (Bullock and Tilley 2003; Pitts 2003). Tim Hope (2003) has argued:

> It is no exaggeration to say that we are now two nations as far as criminal victimisation is concerned. Half the country suffers more than four fifths of the total amount of household property crime, while the other half makes do with the remaining 15 per cent.

The neighbourhoods that experienced the greatest changes during this period were the urban social housing estates, which saw growing concentrations of children, teenagers, young single adults and young single-parent families. The crime in these neighbourhoods is distinctive in several ways. It is:

- *Youthful.* Young people are both victims and perpetrators (Pitts and Hope 1997).

- *Implosive.* Crime is perpetrated by and against local residents (Lea and Young 1988; Wilson 1987; Bourgeois 1995; Palmer and Pitts 2006).

- *Repetitive.* The same people are victimised again and again (Forrester *et al.* 1990).

- *Symmetrical.* Victims and offenders are similar in terms of age, ethnicity and class (Lea and Young 1988).

- *Violent.* The violence is intra-neighbourhood, inter-neighbourhood and often intra-racial (Pitts 2003; Palmer and Pitts 2006).

- *Under-reported.* Victims and perpetrators in the poorest neighbourhoods tend to know one another and the threat of reprisal prevents them from reporting victimisation (Young and Matthews 1992).

- *Embedded.* Youth offending in these areas tends to intensify because, being denied many of the usual pathways to adulthood, adolescents fail to 'grow out of crime' and so the age-range of the adolescent peer group expands, linking pre-teens with offenders in their twenties and thirties (Hagan 1993).

- *Drug related.* In the 1980s opiate use spread from the West End of London to 'dense pockets within our towns and cities … neighbourhoods which are worst affected by unemployment and wretched housing' (Pearson 1988).

- *Gun-enabled.* From the late 1990s, the UK began to experience a sharp rise in firearms-related crime perpetrated by drug-dealing cliques, more often that not in their teens and early twenties. Between 2002 and 2003, for example, firearms offences increased by over 30 per cent (Bullock and Tilley 2003).

In consequence, from the mid 1990s, certain inner-city neighbourhoods and out-of-town estates in London, Birmingham and Manchester developed the types of crime profiles only previously associated with the North American ghetto (Campbell 1993).

From a blag to a business

Meanwhile, higher up the criminal food chain, things were also changing. In London in the 1980s, traditional organised crime, characterised by familial organisations rooted in traditional working-class parochialism, began to give way to 'project crime', a series of temporary collaborations between specialists, in which the link between territorial control and market sovereignty was attenuated, as the neighbourhood was supplanted by the market as the major field of operation (Hobbs and Dunningham 1998). This change was precipitated by the erosion of the traditional white working-class community and the absorption of key local figures into the international trade in illicit opiates.

Traditional organised crime

In their heyday the mobs, like the Kray brothers in east London in the 1960s, exerted control over markets, rackets and neighbourhoods and their influence stretched all the way down to street level. Although they ran quasi-legitimate businesses, like nightclubs, their main income derived from the tribute they received from groups of loosely connected, 'middle-level' professional criminals who perpetrated one-off 'blags' like bank, post office or security van robberies, warehouse thefts and high-value lorry hijacks. In return these 'blaggers' received permission to operate in the territory, inside information about potential targets, the co-operation of 'paid for' criminal justice and local government personnel and access to a network of fences who would buy and distribute their stolen goods.

Mobs like the Kray brothers strove to minimise 'trouble' in their own neighbourhoods in order to keep the police at bay. Thus, ironically, they espoused and enforced conventional behavioural standards in the areas they controlled and this contributed to their considerable local popularity. Indeed it is still possible to find local residents who insist that there would be none of the street crime that now dogs their streets 'if the boys were still about'. And this is not just misplaced nostalgia. In her study of two adjacent Manchester neighbourhoods Sandra Walklate (1999) found that the one dominated by a well-known local criminal family suffered only a fraction of the crime and disorder experienced by the other. These mobs presided over what Cloward and Ohlin (1960) described as an 'organised' as distinct from the 'disorganised slum'.

Ultimately, they were able to exert this level of control because of their reputation for extreme violence. However, this violence was largely instrumental, visited mainly upon other criminals who had 'crossed them'. Many mobsters of this era courted celebrity. They were upwardly aspiring, seeking out relationships with some of the more flamboyant 'establishment' and show business figures, further embellishing their image with high-profile acts of philanthropy.

By the late 1980s, however, improved security and the erosion of the community and familial networks that supported this kind of criminality meant that such artisan crime was becoming less profitable and so the blaggers turned instead to a new and far more lucrative source of easy money; drugs (Hobbs and Dunningham 1998).

The new gangsters

Modern day East End gangland is, by contrast, segmented. In the topmost echelon are the importers and wholesalers the heirs to the old-time gangsters, often involved in variety of illicit markets: drugs, people trafficking, or other contraband, depending upon fluctuations in price and levels of risk. Their illicit enterprises are often integrated with other conventional enterprises and some may be prominent and respected businessmen within their own communities. Whereas the East End mobsters of the 1960s were almost all white British, their modern counterparts come from all over the world, often maintaining 'trade links' with their countries of origin. Indeed in some cases the principals in these illicit businesses live abroad.

Their relationship with the 'middle-market', where the estate-based gangs operate, are temporary and contractual, restricted to the supply of illicit commodities, usually via intermediaries. If these importers and wholesalers do develop face-to-face business relationships, these will be with other upper-echelon operators like themselves, among whom conflict is rare because it is in nobody's interests to 'rock the boat' or attract too much official opprobrium.

Contract compliance problems, when they do arise, tend to involve middle-level dealers, and where the upper-echelon operators need to use force, this is normally contracted out to a disinterested professional, unconnected with either party.

By the late 1990s, heroin and crack cocaine were flooding into London. Four families dominated middle-level drug dealing in Red borough, and four brothers from one of these families, who lived on the Causeway estate, having previously specialised in armed robbery were, like other career criminals of the time, moving into the highly lucrative illicit drugs business. In 2001 the Causeway Gang, backed up by the equally violent Tottenham Man Dem Crew, the Harlesden Crew and, in Hackney, the Love of Money Crew, the Holly Street

Boys and Mothers Square, made a successful bid for control of the East London opiate market and much else besides. As a result, the Causeway Gang, became the major supplier of narcotics in Red borough.

In the wake of these battles the local drugs market stabilised, leading to a sharp reduction in armed violence. Indeed, as recently as 2002 the Metropolitan Police still regarded Red borough as a relatively tranquil place, compared with neighbouring boroughs where drug-driven gang violence was on the rise and, ironically, where control of the Red borough drug market was being decided.

Then, in 2002, a core member of the Causeway Gang was robbed by someone from the Cromwell Drive estate who was, in turn, 'bottled' by the brother of the victim. It is likely that the original robbery was related to a dispute over a drugs deal. In the ensuing conflict the Cromwell Drive Gang became affiliated with three other local estate-based gangs, all of which had 'beefs' (smouldering resentments) with the Causeway Gang, about among other things the way they had muscled in on the drugs business a few years earlier. At this time, these gangs were relatively small, resembling in some respects the criminal networks described by Hallsworth and Young (2004), with core groups of around half a dozen and a handful of associates.

However, the drugs business is a business, requiring a relatively elaborate division of labour within a large workforce, which must maintain and protect the supply chain: market, package and distribute the product, protect the key players, silence would-be whistle-blowers, collect debts and ensure contract compliance. Moreover, it is in the nature of the drugs business that the numbers of people needed to run and protect it will increase until the market reaches saturation point. In consequence, in this period there was a growing demand for young people with the requisite skills and disposition to fill vacancies in this burgeoning illicit labour market. Unfortunately, as a result of structural youth unemployment, school exclusion, which peaked in the early years of the twenty-first century, and truancy, there was no shortage.

Gang structure

Drug-dealing and street crime were a core activity of some of the gangs we studied. Indeed it appeared to be the glue that held them together, generating the money that, along with the violence and their connections into organised crime, enabled them to wield such extraordinary power. Moreover, it appeared that these gangs dictated the style and promulgated the values adopted by other 'gangs' and 'crews' for whom crime was an incidental or marginal activity. So here we describe the structures of those gangs, which 'set the pace', becoming a key cultural reference point for many other young people in the neighbourhoods where they operated (see Figure 5.1).

The crack business in Red borough is dominated by members or close associates of four families. Some senior members of these families had been involved with the Kray brothers in the 1960s and others were said to have links with, or to operate under a franchise

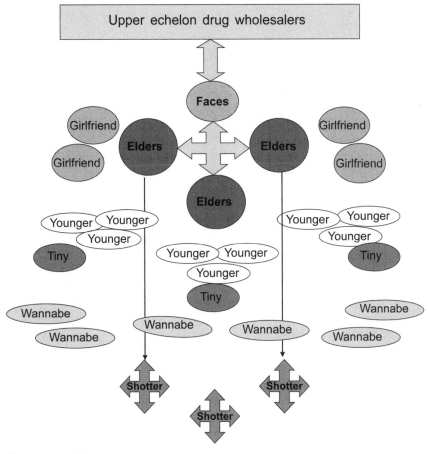

Figure 5.1 Gang structure

arrangement for, the notorious Adams family of north London. These were the Faces, always operating in the background, leaving the higher-profile gang Elders to make reputations for themselves, but also to take the risks that the achievement of such notoriety involves. However, the knowledge that certain gangs were 'connected' to these families was a major factor in the power they are able to wield on the street. In all three boroughs, the larger gangs consisted of a hard core of young men, Elders, usually in their late teens and early twenties.

The Elders were attended by 'crews', small groups of younger boys, variously known as Youngers, Run-arounds, Soldiers or Sabos (derived from 'saboteurs'), usually aged between 14 and 17, who acted as 'foot soldiers' for the gang. To be a Younger is to be an unpaid apprentice or aspirant who is held there by the possibility that one day one might ascend to Elder status and so acquire the kudos, wealth and protection that Elders enjoy. Levitt and Dubner (2005) catch the flavour of this relationship in their chapter entitled 'Why Do Drug Dealers Still Live with Their Moms?':

> So if crack dealing is the most dangerous job in America and if the salary is only $3.30 an hour, why on earth would anyone take such a job? Well, for the same reason that a pretty Wisconsin farm girl moves to Hollywood. For the same reason a high-school quarterback wakes at 5 a.m. to lift weights. They all want to succeed in an extremely competitive field in which, if you reach the top, you are paid a fortune (to say nothing of the attendant glory and power).

Some Elders and Youngers have several young girlfriends (characteristically aged between 13 and 16) who are, apparently, attracted by the 'glamour' and 'celebrity' of gang members. These girls tend to play an ancillary role, sometimes carrying or hiding guns or drugs for the boys. They are often sexually exploited, sometimes in exchange for drugs. The relationship tends to be abusive, with some higher-status gang members passing their 'girlfriends' around to lower-ranking members and sometimes to the whole group. Unreported rape by gang members, as a form of reprisal or just because they can, is said to occur fairly frequently and reports to the police are rare. In Red borough there are some crews of girls, loosely associated with the gangs, who regard themselves as 'soldiers' and concentrate on violent street crime. They do not perform the same sexual role as the 'girlfriends' of gang members. However, recently some Elders in White borough were heard boasting that they have girlfriends who 'go to university' and this may account for the recent spate of 'fly-on-the-wall' dissertations emanating from undergraduate criminology courses.

As we note below, gang Elders make their 'Ps' (money) from drug-dealing – largely skunk, crack cocaine and heroin, which is sold on the street by Shotters. Elders are seldom involved in street robbery, which is regarded as 'petty change' and the province of the smaller, lower-status Crews. The largest gang in White borough also has several legitimate businesses, including a barbershop and a record label. Elders in Red borough appear to direct the activities of the Youngers/Soldiers whose responsibilities include:

- Ensuring drugs get to the Shotters (street dealers).
- 'Hanging out' in the neighbourhood to give early warning of a police presence.
- Patrolling the territorial boundaries of gang estates to protect them from other gangs with a 'beef'.
- Collecting debts for Faces or Elders.
- Taking vengeance and making 'hits' on those who disrespect or cheat them or the Faces or Elders.
- Harassing and burgling rival dealers.
- Undertaking street crime and burglary to raise money for the Elders.

Gang Youngers may deal in drugs or collect the proceeds from drug sales but the money tends to go 'straight up' to the Elders, although some of it may then filter back down again later. The crews of Youngers make most of their money from street crime, although some deal in soft drugs.

Wannabes hover on the fringes of the gang and although they may assume the trappings of street gangs, insignia, street names, etc. and lay claim to territory, they are essentially unrewarded aspirants trying to gain acceptance and eventual inclusion.

Like girlfriends, Youngers and Wannabes may carry weapons, drugs or stolen property for the Elders, to ensure that if the Elders are stopped and searched they will be 'clean' and that no 'forensic' is transferred by direct contact. They may also serve jail terms for them if this proves necessary.

Such is the kudos of the gang in some neighbourhoods that children as young as seven or eight are claiming gang affiliation. Several primary schools in Red borough reported conflict between self-styled gang members and, from time to time, gang-affiliated youngsters from secondary schools are summoned to primary schools by their younger brothers and sisters as reinforcements in the aftermath of an 'inter-gang' playground 'beef'. More recently, however, gang-involved young people and professionals have been talking about Tinys; children of primary school age who are involved on the fringes of gangs and are used to run errands and hide or carry drugs, knives or guns.

A growing market

The 2004 *Red Borough Community Safety and Drug Audit* describes the 'fast-growing' drug trade in the borough, in which 'mergers and acquisitions' facilitated by violence have become commonplace, as a 'high gain/low risk' activity. Recently, however, police action has led to more arrests for opiate-dealing and seizures of the proceeds. However, the borough's police are only able to deal with the drugs trade locally, and because the problem of class A drugs has its origins well beyond the confines of the borough, effective interdiction requires the co-operation of, and hence prioritisation by, national and international policing organisations and Customs and Excise.

The Red borough drugs market: the upper level

Drug markets are segmented. In the topmost echelon are the importers and wholesalers. Some of the crack cocaine that reaches Red borough is smuggled in in large quantities directly from South America by established London crime families and distributed through their networks of 'franchised dealers'. The other source is Jamaica, where the cocaine business is said to constitute 40 per cent of GDP (Silverman 1994; Figueroa and Sives 2002). Cocaine imported from South America to Jamaica, is sometimes processed there and then exported on to the UK, sometimes via West Africa, but almost always in small quantities. Drug mules are the favoured vehicle for this traffic and although the attrition rate in terms of detection and death appears high (for several years African and Caribbean drug mules constituted around 50 per cent of the women in UK gaols), so much gets through that the trade remains highly profitable. Distribution in the UK tends to be handled by local networks, often with familial or nationality links (Silverman 1994) and often via crack houses.

Most heroin used in the UK comes from Afghanistan via Pakistan. The wholesalers are often involved in a variety of illegal markets in drugs, firearms, people and contraband, as well as illicit financial dealings, like 'carousel' VAT fraud. Their enterprises are usually integrated with conventional businesses, and both the money used to finance the deals and the proceeds from them may pass through a labyrinth of legitimate businesses in order to disguise the identities and maintain the security of the principal traders.

Skunk is produced on UK-based 'farms', often located in apparently innocuous suburban houses, while dance drugs are readily available in the night-time economy, sometimes supplied by the security firms charged with keeping the pubs and clubs they 'police' drug-free.

The Red borough drugs market: the middle level

At the next level down are the aforementioned Faces. They are the link between the upper-level drug wholesalers and the street gangs. Jon Silverman (1994) offers a succinct account of how the original middle-level London crack market was developed by the once notorious Face, Sammy Lewis:

> He buys two kilos of cocaine hydrochloride every fortnight from a white guy, who gets it in twenty-five or fifty kilo consignments from God knows who, most probably someone whose home is in Bogota or Caracas. Sammy pays his supplier slightly over the odds, £30,000 per kilo. He can afford to be generous because he 'steps on' or adulterates the powder with other substances so that each kilo stretches a long, long way. So far, in fact, that for every thirty grand he shells out, he gets back at least £65,000, more than doubling his investment. But unlike most of the competition, Sammy converts the powder into washed crack himself rather than selling it on as hydrochloride. He knows that it is crack which brings the heavy-duty returns and he supplies the slabs of magnolia-coloured rock, in two gramme parcels, to each of three dealers who buy regularly from him.
>
> Sammy is the first big wholesaler in London to sell crack in this fashion and he can offer his 'crew', as he calls them, a tempting deal. They buy a parcel for £175 and they can guarantee to double that amount when they sell it on to the street dealer. The crew are happy, they are each making £1,500 a week and

the street sellers aren't complaining either. They recoup their stake from the punters, who will keep buying rocks even if they are only 75 per cent pure, until there is nothing in their wallets but fluff – and then they start stealing for more.

Many of the Elders or Faces involved in the drugs trade at this level have extensive criminal careers and, as we have noted, a penchant for violence (Pearson and Hobbs 2001). In Red borough the Causeway Gang has played this role, selling drugs to other Faces and Elders on other estates, selling to the Shotters, who deal the drugs in the neighbourhoods the gangs control and the surrounding streets, or quite commonly charging Shotters for selling their own drugs in the territories they control and offering the protection of their name in return. The gang-accredited Shotters deal in a variety of drugs, most notably skunk and crack cocaine. Shotters working for, or accredited and protected by, gangs are believed to earn around £300–£500 per week. Shotters work in both 'open' and 'closed' drug markets (May et al. 2005).

Although heroin importation in Red borough is the preserve of South Asian dealers who operate out of storefronts and restaurants, relations between these dealers and the drug-dealing gangs appear to be amicable because it is possible to buy both crack cocaine and heroin from both sources. However, such amicability is possible because the South Asian dealers have the support of a large South Asian gang operating in adjacent boroughs which has a reputation for extreme violence.

Street-level drug markets

Open drug markets

An open drug market is one where, characteristically, several Shotters will sell drugs to anyone willing to buy, unless they are suspected of being police officers or rival gang members. In Red borough they operate on busy thoroughfares adjacent to the estates where the drug-dealing gangs are located, and in the vicinity of underground and overground train stations. The clientele is drawn from all walks of life. An open market has the advantage for buyers that they can retain anonymity and exercise choice between dealers (May et al. 2005). On the other hand, buying from strangers lays the purchaser open to 'rip-offs' and the possibility of robbery because open drug markets in Red borough are also robbery hot spots.

The advantage of an open market for sellers is that it maximises customer access. However, it also renders them vulnerable to police 'buy and bust' tactics and this means that to make a living Shotters must be innovators. When policing intensified in a major thoroughfare in Red borough in 2005, for example, one ingenious Shotter relocated to the rear of the KFC Drive-Through where he supplied crack and heroin to accompany his customer's Colonel Sanders 'Tasty Bites'.

Open markets cannot be protected as effectively as closed markets, and in 2006, rival gangs from an adjacent borough tried to drive out the Red borough Shotters, resulting in several fire-fights. This kind of conflict is, of course, very bad for business, affecting as it does both availability and quality, and making users reluctant to visit these sites. Inter-gang rivalry and police enforcement, if it is sustained, may precipitate a shift from open to closed markets.

Closed drug markets

A closed drug market is one where a Shotter only sells to users who are known to them. Closed markets can be house, car or street based, with contact maintained via mobile phone, but most operate out of premises of some sort. Until police action against them in 2005 and 2006, several closed markets in Red borough were located in 'crack houses', flats that either belonged to gang members or were taken over by them against the wishes of their usually vulnerable owners. Following police action to close down the crack houses in early 2006, some gangs switched to moped/scooter deliveries. However, by the end of the year the crack houses were reappearing.

The economics of a closed drug market

The Cromwell Drive estate (CDE) is a small closed market, in which around 150 people spend a minimum of £50 per week on illicit drugs. Thus the weekly CDE drug-spend is £7,500, or £390,000 a year.

As Tables 5.1a and 5.1b indicate, the Wholesaler and the Elder or Face take the lion's share of the profit but the Shotters also make a reasonable profit from the trade.

Clearly there is a 'good' living to be made from the drugs business at all levels for those with the requisite skills, knowledge and disposition. However, they are inevitably vulnerable to police action.

Table 5.1a Hypothetical weekly cashflow in the Cromwell Drive estate closed drug market

	Buys	Sells	Profit
Wholesaler	1,500	2,500	£1,000
Elder/Face	2,500	5,000	£2,500
Shotters (Dealers) × 5	5,000	7,500	£2,500
Individual Shotter			£ 500

Table 5.1b Hypothetical annual cashflow in the Cromwell Drive estate closed drug market

Wholesaler	£ 52,000
Elder/Face	£130,000
Shotters (Dealers) × 5	£130,000
Individual Shotter/Soldier	£ 26,000

Enforcement and displacement

Sustained police action can seriously disrupt gang-controlled drug markets. We have already noted that dealers may withdraw from open into closed markets in the face of police action. But sustained action can fragment or displace gangs. One key informant in Red borough said that as a result of police action he was now dealing drugs in a Suffolk market town, while two in White borough were dealing in Reading and Cardiff. We heard of others who had shifted their sphere of operations to Liverpool and Manchester, a shift facilitated by pre-existing family and gang links. Police action can also displace gangs into other forms of crime. Following sustained action against their crack houses, for a time the Causeway Elders moved into high-value car-jacking for export in the home counties.

The Caribbean connection

Everybody who knows them recognises that the Causeway Elders have both a capacity and a penchant for violence. However, the extreme violence surrounding their eventual domination of the east London crack market is explicable, in part, by the level of threat posed by their adversaries.

By the late 1970s, Jamaican politics was becoming remarkably violent, as armed gangs associated with the pro-Cuban PNP (People's National Party) and the pro-US JLP (Jamaican Labour Party) battled for electoral supremacy. In the 1980 Jamaican general election the estimated death toll was around 800 (Silverman 1994; Figueroa and Sives 2002; Clarke 2006).

These gangs had their homes in the 'garrison communities', the ghettoes, of Kingston, and in return for their armed support the political parties channelled overseas aid, in the form of improved housing, sanitation, jobs, etc. into these ghettoes. These gangs, known in the UK as Yardies, originally made their living from marijuana sales, but in the early 1980s a successful US-led marijuana suppression programme meant that most gangs switched to the manufacture and sale of crack, derived from cocaine imported from nearby South America. As a result, incomes rocketed, and so did the ferocity and arbitrariness of the associated gang violence.

So violent had these inter-gang struggles become by the late 1980s, and so embattled were these garrison communities, that the PNP and the JLP distanced themselves from the Yardies, and the government of Michael Manley ordered a police crackdown that generated many more fatalities. Seeing the 'writing on the wall' many Yardies, and most notably the Shower Posse, emigrated to areas of Jamaican settlement in the USA, initially becoming street-dealers for the South American drug cartels.

However, such was the Yardies' capacity for extreme violence that very soon they had sidelined the South Americans and moved into wholesale crack supply, eventually opening up new markets in towns like Kansas City, previously untouched by the US crack 'epidemic'. In the struggles between the pro-Cuban PNP and the pro-US JLP in the 1980s some pro-PNP Posses (gangs) from Kingston's garrison communities were spirited away from Jamaica to Cuba for military training, while the CIA is said to have armed the Posses of the JLP, and this was why the combatants in the battles between the garrisons became known as Soldiers. Later, when the Yardies moved to the USA, it was their practice to recruit adolescents from the Kingston ghettoes to low-level roles in the drugs business, in part because juveniles attracted lesser penalties for drug and gun-related crime. Although poorly rewarded for their work, they were granted the title 'Soldier' and held there by the promise of eventual promotion, not unlike the London Soldiers of today.

However, the Yardies eventually became a major focus of the US War on Drugs and they moved on once again, this time to areas of

Jamaican settlement in Canada and the UK. In London from the early 1990s the Yardies, in the guise of the Renkers, the Spanglers and the Gulleymen, were showing up in Hackney, Harlesden, Lambeth, Southwark and Tottenham (Silverman 1994; McLagen 2006).

Gang violence

Although, as Pearson and Hobbs (2001) observe, the drugs business tends to attract career criminals with a penchant for violence, it is in the nature of illicit markets that being unregulated by law, violence, or the threat of violence, becomes the primary means of market regulation (Arlacchi 1998). One of the functions of this violence is to send messages to rival gangs and would-be 'grasses'.

Some things seem too terrible to be true. On one occasion the Causeway Elders kidnapped a man who had crossed them in a drugs deal, stabbed him 17 times and sent the video to his mother. Inevitably, everybody in the locality got to hear about this; indeed, it is unlikely that they will ever forget it. These kinds of incidents are sufficient to silence most would-be whistle-blowers, not least because of the widespread belief that 'the authorities' would be unable to protect them if they did break their silence.

Much of the apparently irrational and excessive violence surrounding the drugs business is instrumental, designed to 'get the job done', and not simply reducible to the psychological proclivities of individual gang members. As one respondent said of a group of gang members who had been charged with several counts of attempted murder:

> I grew up with them. Some of them were really nice blokes, but that's just the drugs business, everyone does it. It's kind of expected. It's terrible but these blokes aren't nutters.

Several other respondents pointed to the discrepancy between the apparent normality of some senior gang figures and the horrifying acts of violence they sometimes committed or commissioned. This is not to deny, however, that gangs also attract some very disturbed and dangerous individuals.

Gun crime

Since the late 1990s, gun crime perpetrated by young gang members has escalated in the major cities of England and Wales (Bullock and Tilley 2003). This is in large part a result of greater availability and falling prices. A youth worker interviewed in White borough in July 2007 said:

> The road is getting harder and more dangerous and nobody will stand for being 'dissed' any more. More 10 to 17-year-olds are getting involved in gun crime and the price is falling. You can now buy a gun for as little as £50–£100.

Another White borough practitioner, interviewed in September 2007, noted that one of the reasons the work was becoming more dangerous was the appearance on the streets of the 'Spray and Pray' Mach 10 semi-automatic machine gun.

The price of firearms is determined in part by whether the gun is 'clean' or 'dirty'. A Red borough gang member interviewed in October 2006 said:

> You can get a clean [unused] gun for £600 and a dirty [used] one for £200 or £300.

According to him, demand is particularly high among younger, wannabe gang members on a particular Red borough estate:

> Five kids, aged about 14 and 15 were all clubbing together to get their own gun. They're all putting in £50. Everyone wants one.

There are cheaper alternatives, however. Another young Red borough respondent said:

> Renting a gun don't cost much but it's dangerous – you don't know where it's been.

This awareness of incriminating forensic residues is also expressed in the gang dress code.

> **JP:**   Why are you all wearing gloves?
> **Danny:** To hurt people when you punch them or to be ready if someone pulls a gun or a knife.

JP: *What do you mean, 'ready'?*
Danny: *Say someone pulls up in a car and they've already got a gun out or they come at you with a knife. You haven't got time to get your gloves on, so you're gonna get forensic or blood or something on your hands.*

In the two years from 1 January 2005 to 31 December 2006 there were 493 incidents of gun-enabled crime in Red borough, 275 in 2005 and 218 in 2006 (CRIS data, 2007). The term 'gun-enabled crime' covers everything from threats with a replica firearm to wounding and death.

Table 5.2 shows that it is primarily a pursuit of those under 20, that African-Caribbean children and young people are heavily over-represented as perpetrators, and that perpetrators are overwhelmingly male. If we turn to the victims of gun-enabled crime, once again we

Table 5.2 Gun-enabled crime in Red borough

Ages of perpetrators	Percentage (average)
1–10	11
11–20	53
21–30	30
Ethnicity of perpetrators	
White Caucasian	18
Black African Caribbean	59
Asian	10
Gender of perpetrators	
Male	92
Female	5
Ages of victims	
1–10	19
11–20	27
21–30	27
Ethnicity of victims	
White Caucasian	39
Black African Caribbean	31
Asian	13
Gender of victims	
Male	69
Female	30

find an over-representation of African-Caribbean youngsters but also a far larger number of white Caucasian children and young people.

Particularly striking is the number of children under ten and the large number of girls and young women who are victimised in this way. While between 2 per cent and 5 per cent of gun-crime suspects in Red borough are young women, they constitute around 30 per cent of gun crime victims. Unsurprisingly perhaps, gun-enabled crime in Red, White and Blue boroughs is concentrated in or near to the major gang estates and overlaps with street crime and drug-dealing hot spots.

These figures underline the fact that while the overall volume of gun-enabled crime in Britain has increased in the recent period, those involved both as victims and as perpetrators are becoming younger and that young women and girls are more likely than ever before to be victimised. As yet we know little about why this should be, but because of the violence and the sexual abuse and exploitation to which young women are subject in gangland, it is clear that engagement with them must be a priority for any strategy developed to combat gang crime.

Chapter 6

We are family: gang cultures

The most dangerous creation of any society is the man who has nothing to lose.

James Baldwin, *Nobody Knows My Name* (1962)

When you find a friend
Who is good and true
Fuck him
Before he fucks you

J.P. Donleavy (2006)

Introduction

Gang affiliation is complex. Some young people may embrace life in the gang because it appears to offer the inclusion, success and protection otherwise denied them. Others are fatalistic, drifting into affiliation because for them the gang is the 'only game in town'. These are the young people we discuss in this chapter. In the next chapter we consider those other young people whose affiliation is reluctant: a product of fear, constraint or coercion.

The young people involved in violent youth gangs seldom use the term; speaking instead of 'family', 'breddrin', 'crews', 'coz' (cousins), 'my boys' or simply, 'the people I grew up with'. Whatever they are called they are distinguishable by what they do and what they say they think about what they do.

Gang culture

Culture is at once a distinctive heritage, the means whereby people differentiate themselves from others, a collective response to a changing world and a defining feature of who we are. Culture is dynamic not static, it is constantly incorporating new elements and discarding the old, and for this reason it can be difficult at any given time to pin down exactly what 'gang' or 'street' culture actually is. Nonetheless, listening to gang-involved young people it is possible to develop some understanding of what is distinctive, and sometimes where this distinctiveness comes from.

Some commentators have suggested that twenty-first century UK gangs are a product of the Americanisation or globalisation of youth culture, via MTV, films and music (Young 1999), and this influence is clearly evident among the Red, White and Blue borough gangs. However, not only does this view tend to overstate the role of popular culture while understating the contribution of socio-structural factors, it also ignores the reality that youth cultures are elaborate constructions; representing the convergence, and transformation, of many diverse influences. In Red borough, as we have seen, some gangs have a history that stretches back to the last days of the Kray brothers and connections that reach into multinational criminal business organisations.

The Kingston connection

In his survey of European gangs Malcolm Klein (1996) observed that English gangs were distinctive because unlike their European counterparts they bear a strong resemblance, in terms of their structure and culture, to 1980s US crack-dealing gangs. It may therefore be that elements of contemporary gang culture in London can be traced back to the armed gangs that originated in the 'garrison communities' of Kingston, Jamaica in the 1970s (Clarke 2006).

The impact of the gang cultures that surfaced in Kingston in the 1960s upon twenty-first century English street culture is considerable. As we have seen, the gangsters known as Yardies came to Britain from the garrison communities of Kingston, via the USA, in the 1990s, and some of the practices they brought with them have become key reference points for gang-affiliated young people.

This influence can be seen in the music and the language of contemporary street culture; in the fact that Youngers in the Red,

White and Blue boroughs, like an earlier generation of Jamaican adolescents working in the American crack business, are known as Soldiers; in friendship patterns, gender relations and gang structures. It is evident in the nature and severity of the violence some of the gangs and crews perpetrate, and in the level of control they endeavour to exert over the neighbourhoods they claim as their own.

As we noted in Chapter 5, the migration of Yardie gangsters from the USA to England in the 1990s transformed both the style and substance of the drugs business and intensified the violent struggles within it. However, present-day youth gang culture in London is not simply an emulation of Yardie culture. Strong links exist between some of the gangs in the garrison communities of Kingston and families, criminal networks and youth gangs in London, and protagonists in both countries are sometimes as familiar with the goings on in Brixton and Peckham as they are with the action in Kingston's Trenchtown and Southside.

In Kingston, each garrison community has its own 'sound', and gang members are involved in producing 'beats' containing both positive political messages and threats and insults directed against their adversaries. Following the exodus of the Jamaican Yardies from the USA, Robert Blackwood (aka Rankin Dread, aka Bowyark), senior gunman with the Shower Posse and successful recording artist, who previously controlled the pro-JLP Rema garrison in Kingston, resurfaced at the head of a drug-dealing and armed robbery gang in Hackney. Far from detracting from his stature as a recording artist, being so 'bad' apparently served to enhance it.

There is, of course, a danger of overstating these cultural connections, but it is significant that Billy Cox, the part Thai part white, 15-year-old shot dead in Clapham on Valentine's Day 2007 was described by his friends as a 'fallen soldier'. He used the tag 'Remer', a misspelling of the street name for Wilton Gardens in downtown Kingston, the stamping ground of Robert Blackwood's Shower Posse. Nor is it a coincidence that Peckham, south London, boasts its own Shower Posse and its feminine counterpart, the Shower Chicks.

The major White borough gang has a music production arm, producing and marketing CDs of their albums. They tend to be dedicated to this activity and will go to the West End of London to sell their albums from rucksacks. They also throw a number of raves and take over venues in order to ensure that they can perform, usually accompanied by their own film crew. Robberies are sometimes filmed and used to promote their music. Despite the quality of their 'beats', they find it impossible to get record deals because of the extreme violence and misogyny expressed by their lyrics.

Music is also central to the lives of gang members in Red borough. Here too the lyrics carry threats and insults directed against rival gangs. In 2006 one such beat, said to have 'dissed' a rival gang member, provided the pretext for a fatal attack.

Street life

In gang-affected neighbourhoods, the influence of street culture is present from an early age. Buster (18), from Blue borough, said:

> *When I was a kid he [his brother] had a lot of friends who sold drugs and they were round my house, and I went out with them sometimes and I saw them do things, I see them robbing people, selling drugs, see them making a lot of money. I was like five, me and my brothers are very close.*

One primary school headteacher in White borough said that children on the estate served by her school had become inured to the gangs, guns, drug-dealing and violence around them. She described a police raid on the estate. As armed police crouched behind cars and street furniture, the children walked past the cordoned-off area, apparently oblivious to the unfolding drama only yards away. She was concerned that these children were growing up believing that this way of life was 'normal'. Primary school staff said that sometimes children would talk about who was in which gang, the weapons they carried and the money they were making from drug sales.

Involvement in street culture normally presented itself as a choice when young people started secondary school. Some young people flirted with street culture, adopting only the style of dress and the mode of speech. For them it was just a 'phase', but nonetheless a phase that carried many dangers. Others become more heavily involved. Many of these young people appeared to believe that there was no alternative for them and 'no way back' from involvement in street culture. Many, but by no means all, had been brought up in poverty and their life chances were often further truncated by criminal convictions, truancy or school exclusion; all of which served to erode their capacity to survive and achieve in the educational and vocational mainstream.

Street culture and the school

Many young, gang-involved, men and women appeared to have gained little from, and had often felt marginalised within, the schools they attended. In some cases this was associated with a belief that institutional routes to success were either unavailable to them because of racism or class prejudice, or if they were available, would require them to make a choice between the institution, in which they had achieved little success and did not feel valued, and the 'street', where with luck and the right connections they could build respect and achieve status.

Respondents in the parental focus groups traced these attitudes among black students to the experiences of an older generation of black men, many of whom had experienced failure and humiliation at school and as a result, had either rejected or developed a profound scepticism about the viability of institutional routes to success.

This fostered a situation in which 'dropping out' or being excluded from school emerged as a 'cool' option for black young people and 'going solo', being self-sufficient and taking care of business 'on your own', with the 'odds stacked against you', came to be viewed as the way to retain self-respect and the respect of others. This inversion and rejection of conventional values may also explain the importance ascribed to being 'bad' (as opposed to 'good').

This obviously created a dilemma for those young people who did want to succeed at school. A headteacher in Red borough said that young people of African or African-Caribbean origin were caught in a double bind in some schools: they would be 'shamed' by the other children if they gave wrong answers in class or achieved low marks, but if they consistently gave right answers or achieved high marks, they would be ridiculed as a 'boff' (boffin) or a 'neek' (nerd/geek). This, she said, tended to generate or support a student culture in which academic success was juxtaposed with 'street' success, with boys, in particular, adopting an anti-academic 'cool pose' (Bowling and Phillips 2006).

Street crime

Violent street crime is how the Youngers or Soldiers 'earn their Ps', and while it funds a lifestyle that may involve purchasing drugs, it is not drug-driven (May *et al.* 2005). Young people involved in street culture grow accustomed to the idea that although their access to legitimate opportunities may be blocked, money can be acquired quickly and easily from street robbery. The more deeply a young person becomes involved in street culture, the greater their financial needs become, because having status on the streets means being seen to have money and being seen to spend it on your 'crew', 'boys', 'gang' or 'family', and in some cases, 'to put food on the table' for your family of origin or a new family in which you are a parent. As a result, the more they become involved in street culture, the less likely they are to be attracted by the modest rewards of the few legitimate jobs available to them.

Because of this, 'street crime careers' tend to escalate. Figure 6.1, constructed on the basis of interviews with young people involved in street crime in Blue borough, characterises this escalation. Robbery is often just the first rung on a ladder that can lead to involvement in drug-dealing, which for some may lead on to involvement in organised crime, with the attendant risk of serious injury or death. Joel (19), from Blue borough, said:

Target	Motivation	Rationale
1 *Members of the public*	To get ready cash ('quick eats').	'They can afford it.'
2 *'Friends'*	To get ready cash and/or re-establish your position in the hierarchy.	'He/She's got it, I haven't'. 'It keeps them in their place.'
3 *Rival groups/gangs/ crews*	To establish or re-establish respect/ street-status and/or resolve a 'beef.'	'If I don't do it to them they'll do it to me.'
4 *Drug-dealers/shotters*	To make 'serious money'.	'I'm too old for street street crime and need to establish myself in the criminal hierarchy.'

Figure 6.1 A typology of street robbery

People move up once they realise there is nothing in street robberies, when there is more in armed robberies and drug dealing. Someone my age, who has people below him who can do things for him.

Street crime may be instrumental, but it is also a means whereby Youngers assert their power and authority in the street to gain recognition and 'respect' (Young 1999; Sanders 2004; Wright *et al.* 2006), and this is why so much street robbery is perpetrated against members of other gangs or crews or their friends and relatives.

Early results from the Edinburgh Study of Youth Transitions and Crime (McAra 2006) suggest that in high-crime neighbourhoods being a victim of crime at the age of 12 is a powerful indicator that a child will be offending at age 15. This could be, as some academics have suggested, that victims and perpetrators share similar personality traits (McAra 2006). However, as we found and other studies suggest, in certain low socio-economic status neighbourhoods children and young people with low or no familial or personal 'risk factors' may be significantly more prone to gang involvement and gang victimisation because of the risks present within their neighbourhoods (Sampson and Laub 1993; Hagan 1993; Wikstrom and Loeber 1997).

Street culture is a powerful influence, but not just upon young people with troubled backgrounds and few prospects. Some respondents who were heavily involved in street culture came from stable families and had achieved academic success. Buster (18), from Blue borough, had 11 GCSEs and had recently graduated from straightforward street crime to robbing drug-dealers. Delroy started out doing street robberies in Blue borough and moved on, via a gang, to more serious forms of crime. He also had good GCSEs, plus three A levels and had just started at university. He was also running a crack business that yielded £1,500 a week:

It is something that I didn't expect, like once you do something, you get deeper and deeper into things. It is fast cash, easy money, tax free.

However, even the most street-smart operator in this dangerous world is likely, one day, to 'come unstuck'. Buster said:

On the streets anything could happen, any time, so it's not a new thing – you're not surprised if people are shot or shanked. You can't go through the street life without being stabbed or beaten. Something will eventually happen to you.

This constant exposure to violence, their awareness of the precarious nature of life and the 'soldier mentality' discussed in Chapter 3 means that these young people have great difficulty envisaging a life that extends beyond their twenties. And the fatalism engendered by this bleak perspective, elevates 'respect' to a paramount virtue.

Violence and respect

A recent study of street crime by Richard Wright and colleagues (2006) confirms that much of it is primarily concerned with respect and recognition rather than simple monetary gain. Gang members in Red and White boroughs would sometimes video their offences and post them on websites. While this rendered them more vulnerable to prosecution, it also demonstrated their contempt for the law and as such served to consolidate their reputation for toughness, and hence the 'respect' in which they were held.

As gangs grow larger and more powerful, respect-based conflict becomes more common. The incidents that trigger this conflict may appear trivial and disproportionate, yet gangland is an intensely parochial and inward-looking place with a hyperactive, but not always wholly reliable, grapevine.

I came out of [young offender institution] and there were these six boys on the XXXX estate who wanted to fight me because of something I was supposed to have said when I was inside. You have to fight otherwise you'd look scared and it would get worse and they would think they could do what they like with you. They have to know that it won't be easy.

Respect matters because to be disrespected is to be 'fair game' for anyone who wants to make a name for themselves, and this is virtually everybody involved with gangs. And this is also, as Bill Sanders (2004) notes, why in certain neighbourhoods being 'mugged' is often a prelude to a career of street crime, as young people endeavour to rebuild respect in their social milieu in the wake of an attack. However, being respected in this way has a particularly acute downside. Ronan in Red borough said:

Respect? Well, it's fear isn't it. You want to be feared, but nobody is untouchable, there is always someone to come after you with a blade or something. There's no way out.

Many gang members appear to have a virtually obsessional pre-occupation with status and respect. This is institutionalised into gang culture in the form of an elaborate non-verbal and clothing-based etiquette, the breach of which 'can get you killed'. And this preoccupation is spreading.

Deadly symbiosis

In his book *Deadly Symbiosis*, Loïc Wacquant (2004) writes:

> Along with racial division, the predatory culture of the street, centered on hypermasculine notions of honor, toughness, and coolness has transformed the social structure and culture of jails and prisons. The 'convict code,' rooted in solidarity among inmates and antagonism towards guards has been swamped by the 'code of the street,' with its ardent imperative of individual 'respect' secured through the militant display and demonstrated readiness to mete out physical violence.

It appears that this subcultural cross-pollination is now occurring in the UK.

> Jail watchdogs have warned that an influx of rival gang members from Britain's inner cities has fuelled a new wave of fear and violence at the five maximum security prisons. A new generation, who have been schooled in street, gun and gang culture, bring with them deeply held gang allegiances. Once inside, they use all their ingenuity to equip themselves with home-made, but nevertheless lethal, weapons to settle scores with rival gang members and protect their illicit trade in drugs and mobile phones. (*Guardian*, 23 January 2008)

The erosion of solidarity

Many commentators have argued that because in post-industrial societies consumption has become a primary source of identity, the socially disadvantaged are exposed to intense pressure to fulfil escalating media-driven material expectations (see, for example, Young 1999; Hallsworth 2005). While they are culturally included in the sense that they share mainstream material aspirations, they are economically excluded, being denied the means to fulfil these aspirations through legitimate channels. It is this sense of relative deprivation, they argue, that drives street crime. But while this is probably true, it does not explain why similarly disadvantaged young people from the same locality, with a shared ethnicity, cultural heritage and personal history, visit sometimes lethal violence upon one another.

Ace (17), from Blue borough, explains:

It is not just people robbing any old women on the street, they are robbing their so-called 'friends' or the so-called 'breddrins', the same people rob each other because they think we're in the same situation.

Interviewees said that while there is plenty of money around 'friendships are possible', but when the money runs out 'friends' are quite likely to turn on one another. On the street and around the neighbourhood, friendships and affiliations tend to be short term and pragmatic.

While robbing friends may simply be about money it can also be a way of reaffirming, or rearranging, the pecking order within gangs, and this accounts in part for their fluidity and volatility.

Parents in a Blue borough focus group contrasted this way of being with the solidaristic peer group relations they enjoyed when they were young. This echoes the views of adult respondents on a north-west London housing estate interviewed by Suzella Palmer (2008). They believed that crime among the younger generation had become more random, spontaneous and localised, in that both the perpetrators and victims of these predations were more often than not, drawn from the immediate neighbourhood. Moreover, they said that this violent crime appeared to be less instrumental than in the past, concerned with wounding and robbing people to gain respect and status rather than just acquiring possessions or money. Ryan, a first-generation respondent who has lived in the neighbourhood for over 30 years, bemoaned the fact that:

Half of the shootings that have happened over the last 10 years – do you know that the parents of the kids that have been shooting each other was boyfriend and girlfriend or close friends?

Jason, a third-generation respondent from the same estate, said:

I've been set up a few times but I'm not watching no faces because that's life. You don't know the brers ... face covered, it might be your own friends.

For many, exposure to this dangerous 'dog-eat-dog' world begins in secondary school. 'Young Blade' (16), from Blue borough, said:

When I started reaching secondary school, that's when I started to see boys get robbed, boys like me, black boys, get robbed. I was like 11 or 12, big boys spitting in other boys' faces. It was nice in primary school but it suddenly got worse and then the years after it got worse, people start dying. This is why people are dying – everyone is for theirself, they don't care about this and that so I don't trust no one. I trust myself and my mum and my freedom.

Many of the young people caught up in this anarchic world expressed a possibly ill-founded nostalgia for a time when conflict on the streets was rule-governed. OJ (19) said:

Those rules died ages ago, man no one does one-on-one any more ... each time a one-on-one starts then people come straight in and start scrapping bruv and then the shanks are out ... then it comes back to you.

Money, masculinity and menace

2008 saw the birth of a new, pan-London gang called All About Money (ABM). And at one level, it is all about money. Real men make real money. Money is frozen desire, the commodification of everything that was ever missing from their young lives; it's the way they keep score; the way they know how valuable they are. The ability to amass, hold on to and take money from other people is the pre-eminent source of respect in gangland and this respect is their ultimate validation. It's something worth dying for.

Yet, as Suzella Palmer (2008) has shown, far from enabling these young people to transcend their social marginality, their money bolsters a 'ghetto fabulous' lifestyle of designer sportswear, Rolex watches, 'smoked-out, Mercs', expensive champagne and the purest crack. This is, as Smith (1997) has observed, a lifestyle that provides 'a sense of purposeful presence where previously there may have been only shame, despair, and the urge to fade away,' not an escape.

On the face of it, the enormous amounts of money generated by the drugs trade should enable the Elders and Faces to lead the celebrity lifestyles to which they apparently aspire: a house in the hills above Antibes, a yacht on Montego Bay, etc. Such aspirations are fuelled in part by MTV but also by the fact that many football stars come from gang-affected neighbourhoods and are related or known personally to some gang members. However, three main factors work against the attainment of such 'glittering prizes'. First, the reputation, status, contacts and loyalties that enable senior gang members to dominate their areas are essentially local. To abandon the gang and move to another area would be to become a 'nobody', albeit a very rich one, in an alien social world. And this suggests that the 'recognition' that flows from being a local 'big shot' is as important as the money they make from it. Second, many Elders not only sell crack cocaine, they also use it; the chaos this generates in their lives militates against the financial planning that would enable them to realise such lofty aspirations.

JP: *So where does all the money go, then?*
Del: *I dunno, it just goes … clubbing, drugs, mates, girls, taxis, more drugs, mates, girls, going out … it just goes.'*
JP: *Do they enjoy themselves?*
Del: *I dunno, they've got a brand new Merc outside but they're cracked-out in some poxy flat with their mum. They can't use the front room in case someone shoots the house up, and they're looking at untold 'bird' if they get nicked. What's that about?*

Third, it is one thing to be a big shot in the gang, profiting from the protection it affords, but quite another to leave it.

The illicit acquisition of these prized symbols of success is a bid for 'respect' in a situation where the day-to-day experience of schooling, policing, and living in an area of disrepute among people regarded as 'losers' denies them that respect. Moreover in this world respect and masculinity are indissoluble and the more tenuous their hold on the 'glittering prizes' of conventional life, the more problematic their sense of personal and gender identity becomes (Messerschmidt 1993). As Jock Young observes:

Young men facing such a denial of recognition turn … to the creation of cultures of machismo, (specifically) to the mobilisation of one of their only resources, physical strength, to the formation of gangs and to the defence of their own 'turf'. Being denied the respect of others they create a subculture that revolves around masculine powers and 'respect'. (Young 1999: 12)

And this is one reason why, as Cloward and Ohlin (1960) observed nearly half a century ago in their 'disorganised slum', as the social and economic predicament of the young men worsens, the targets of their predations are likely to become other young men just like themselves, from neighbourhoods just like theirs.

Chapter 7

Reluctant gangsters

He said, 'When you see us together you think we are all friends, don't you Miss, but we're not.'

Headteacher, Blue borough

David's story

I was 13 when we moved to the Matisse estate in Blue borough. At first I just stayed in and it was a long time before I made any friends. I used to go down to the internet café and one day I met this older kid, he was about 21, and after a while he said why didn't I 'hang' with him and his friends.

Where I was before [on an estate in another London borough] sometimes there was a lot of talk, like people saying I had said things about people and so on, but the worst that could happen there was that maybe four or five people might rush me, using their fists and feet. They weren't nearly as violent as this new lot but I didn't see that at first.

Down in Blue borough it seemed more relaxed at first, none of this talking about each other all the time and so I failed to notice that it was a war zone. But then I saw some fights and they were really violent. These fights were between kids from our estate, Matisse, and three others: Gauguin, Dali and Van Gogh. People would be stabbed, I saw five people stabbed during the two years I was there and I heard of two more Olders who died after being stabbed. A lot of kids got stabbed but it never got into the newspapers. But as I saw it most of these fights were about nothing, just about money and things. Sometimes I was there with them but I didn't know what to do, I couldn't tell them to stop or they would have turned on me. You watch and learn – I got used to it in the end. My Older, the one I met in the internet café, was the one doing most of the stabbing and shooting. After I'd left the estate I heard he shot someone dead in a car. But he looked out for me, the group could have turned on me at any time because I didn't have other friends to turn to, so he protected me.

I realised that if you lived there [on the estate] you couldn't ignore what was happening because they would turn against you. You had to be part of it. I reckon about 200 of the 300 kids on the estate were involved with the gang. It was like being in a family; you couldn't avoid being in it and if you were in it you had to contribute to it. Contributing to it meant either selling drugs or fighting. You could also contribute legally, like helping to promote the music that some of the kids made, if you had the skills, but most of these kids didn't have the skills and didn't earn any money. Mind you, three of them were at university. I think because they'd grown up there the culture was too strong for them to leave. Others were in school or college although most were out of school.

But the problem is, once you get in you can't get out, and if you live on one of the gang estates, you're in, full stop. This means that if you go to another gang area and they recognise you, you can be killed. If they don't recognise you you'd just be robbed. So it's not only pressure from your own gang but also the threat from the other gangs that means that if you are part of it you can't leave it. There really is no way out unless you go a long way away, like back to Jamaica with your parents or something.

In the gang there were Tinys, some as young as seven but mainly around 10 or 12; Unclassifieds, like I was, aged 13 to 15; Youngers aged 15 to 18; and Olders aged 18 up to 30. The Tinys were mainly into football and fun although sometimes they would go by bus to have fist-fights with the Tinys on Gauguin, Dali and Van Gogh. That's how it was, Tinys on Tinys, Youngers on Youngers and Olders on Olders.

Our lot on Matisse were mainly either African Caribbeans or Somalis. But they weren't Somalis from Somalia, most of them had come from Holland. I think there are lots of Somali gangs in Holland. On the Gauguin they were mainly African Caribbean, White and Arabs, the Dali was mostly Africans and the Van Gogh was Muslims: some Asian, some African.

The money came mainly from selling drugs. The Youngers would sell cannabis, while the Olders would sell crack cocaine and heroin.

I heard they got it from Somalia but I don't know how. They would sell it right out on the street by the flats; everybody knew. The Olders would give money to the Youngers, even though they deceived the Olders about how much they were earning from the cannabis, and then the Youngers would give us money and we were supposed to give it to the Tinys. I wouldn't take it because I knew that accepting drug money could get you into real trouble. So I guess that a 14-year-old Unclassified involved in dealing was clearing around £300 a month while the Youngers were taking £1,000 a month. The Olders were making much more. But giving away all this money was really an investment for the Olders because at some point they were going to ask the kids to do something illegal or dangerous for them and they would have to do it.

Most of the parents didn't know anything about any of this though, because the kids would leave all the expensive clothes and things in an abandoned house near the estate. There was all sorts there: clothes, drugs, computers, guns; I saw an AK47 in there once, I think it was real, they said it had come from Somalia. There were lots of guns around but most of them weren't new so after they'd used them they would have to get rid of them so they couldn't be traced.

Kids think guns, and shooting someone or being shot, are very glamorous. They don't have any sense of the future. They take every day as it comes; they're always ready for action. There are heartless people who might just shoot you for the 'rush'. But if the guy's got that mentality, you have to think like that too or you'd be dead. This is why it grows. Most people involved in gangs would rather be doing something else. A lot of the time they're just keeping the others sweet so they don't get hurt.

Their lives revolve around money. Money gets you respect, and being able to hang on to your money or take it off other people, violently, gets you even more respect. And that was the bit I didn't get. I want to start my own business doing computer graphics and design, I want to do something constructive with my life, but for them it was all just 'money' and 'respect'.

The extreme violence is about pride or respect which is very important to these guys and these feuds have been going for a long time and so they build up and build up. If they come and attack your estate they might even go into your house. One kid, they went after him in his house and beat up his mum and turned over his baby brother's cot and threw the baby on to the floor. Sometimes they would kidnap people and lock them in some place just because they could. They seemed to have no idea of the consequences of what they were doing.

99

HARPER COLLEGE LIBRARY
PALATINE, ILLINOIS 60067

There are white kids in some of the gangs. Black kids usually think white kids are too feeble; not on the same level either physically or mentally. So the white kids in gangs are basically white kids who grew up with black kids and share their culture and standards. The only thing White about them is the colour of their skin. You can tell by the way they walk and talk and the way they think. Black people's thinking is deeper than white people's. While white people will suppress their deepest thoughts, black people will come right out with them.

The night I got arrested we all set off on the bus and I heard we were going to have a fight with the Racist Attackers, white boys from another area. I never saw any weapons. But even before we were off the bus two people from the Van Gogh had been stabbed and one had been beaten up with a golf club. So then we were just hanging about nearby when the police came. There were about 60 of us and they arrested 21 people – the ones who didn't run fast enough. They charged me with GBH and Violent Disorder but then they dropped the GBH, probably because the CCTV shows me on a bus that hadn't arrived there till after the stabbings. But they're doing me for Joint Enterprise because someone who was there phoned my mate while we were on the bus.

Usually, the police didn't do much. They might search you and find a knife and then let you keep it and not charge you. We thought they did this so that we would go and kill some other gang kid and solve their problem for them. I heard the local police even beat up stabbed people in the police van. There was one copper, we called him Robber Robs, who would take the money off the kids selling drugs and let them carry on dealing. The other trick was to pick up gang kids on the Matisse, for example, give them a hard time in the van, and then sling them out on the Van Gogh, knowing that they could be stabbed and possibly killed. There were fights with the police but sometimes nobody was arrested. They'd wait till they had a really serious charge and then do lots of people. We really hated them and they hated us. I think the police are probably different in other areas but it was bad down there.

The gang thing isn't just local. Like I wouldn't go to East London, that would be too dangerous. West London's OK because I've got family there. But I wouldn't go to South-west London, or Kilburn, Harrow, Wembley or Kensal Rise. I might go to Brixton, shopping, but not on my own. If you go on your own you can get robbed. If you go with a little crew that could spark a fight with another gang, so it's best to go with just one friend. Even if you're in the wrong area with your mum, they'll still try and get you.

Where I am now, they have fights but these are sort of organised and refereed so that nobody gets badly hurt. I don't have anything to do with that, though; I just do my course and hang out in friends' houses. Now and again some boys might give me the look or something, but because of what I learnt on the Matisse estate, they soon get the idea that they should leave me alone.

Do I miss it? No, I don't!

David is like many young people we met in Red, White and Blue boroughs whose gang affiliation was prompted, first and foremost, by a concern for their personal safety. We describe them as 'reluctant gangsters'. David, a mature, intelligent, physically strong and personable young man, was recruited because he had skills and attributes that made him attractive to senior gang members. There were, as David observes, other young people on his estate who were not approached as he was. The reasons for this are as complex as the reasons for affiliation, but it seems that race and ethnicity, gender, family connections, reputation, and perceptions of personal attributes and style are key. However, as with 'Joes' in prisons, notionally unaffiliated young people can be asked to undertake one-off tasks for gang members, which they would be unlikely to refuse, knowing the kind of retribution that refusal was likely to incur. Putting it another way, in gangland, everybody is a potential affiliate.

Joint enterprise

A Youth Offending Team (YOT) worker in Red borough commented that some children and young people coming to the YOT for gang-related crime:

... have no previous record; they're good school attendees and have a good attitude. But they are coming into the YOT for 'joint enterprise' because they were present at the scene. One of our 15-year-olds is doing ten years for attempted murder. It was his knife but everyone knows it was his Elder that did it. They even do time for them.

These young people are reluctant affiliates, whose gang involvement is essentially pragmatic, a means of securing some degree of safety in high-risk situations. Data from a YOT caseload survey undertaken in Red borough, and interviews with young people, indicated that the gang involvement of over one-third of these young people was either involuntary or constrained in some way. This data suggested six modes of reluctant affiliation.

I Affiliation because of the risks to oneself and one's family

According to one YOT worker:

> Some kids say they were made to do things by Elders. Many of them don't necessarily approve of what they are doing. Most kids would rather be doing something else. But gang culture prevents participation. They are frightened of becoming the target of violence.

If the local gang asks someone on the estate to do something, like a street robbery, they know they must do it or suffer the consequences. A social worker said:

> There were a brother and a sister; he was 15 and she was 14. Never been in trouble. They told them to do a robbery. But they said no. So they beat him up and raped her.

In these circumstances neutrality or disaffiliation is exceptionally difficult. A local resident observed:

> If you are not with a gang you are at the bottom of the hierarchy and you'd be very vulnerable.

Speaking of a neighbour's son who stood out against gang affiliation, one informant said:

> He's 18 and he won't ever come out of his house. He says it's more than his life's worth.

Even if a young person has the strength to stand out against gang affiliation, the reprisals may be against their family. One local resident said:

> So he tells 'em to 'fuck off'. Anyway, the next thing he knows, someone's shot-up his mother's flat. There's lots of families round here can't use their front rooms because of this sort of thing.

2 Affiliation because of the risk from other gangs

The earliest US gang studies (Thrasher 1929) found that gangs were brought together and held together by fear of other gangs. And 70 years on Decker and Van Winkle (1996) described how threats from the neighbourhood gang, and rival gangs, induce young people to join. As the gangs in the Red, White and Blue boroughs grew larger, in the early years of the twenty-first century, and territorial disputes intensified, the numbers of protagonists increased and it was no longer easy to distinguish who, on any given estate, was or wasn't a gang member. This meant that, in effect, residence became synonymous with affiliation and young people with no prior gang involvement were restricted to their own estates because of the threat posed to them by rival gangs. One gang member, 'Markeyman', said:

People would come up to you and say, 'Where are you from?' And if you said the wrong area they would have you – but you don't always know what to say.

In this situation of profound mutual fear and suspicion generated by the conflict, rumours abounded and respect-related attacks escalated. Kevin, a 16-year-old gang member, said:

There was this gossip about some girl and so I was supposed to have a fight with this one boy. But about 10 or 20 of his gang come round from the XXXX with metal poles. So I jumped back in my house and I rung my boys and they come down and we chased them off.

This increasingly dangerous environment served as a stimulus for many previously unaffiliated young people to join their local gang as a means of self-defence but also to arm themselves with knives and sometimes guns. Yet, such was the threat posed by the gangs that even young people who had previously held out against affiliation could now be pressurised into undertaking illegal tasks if gang members required them to do so.

From the summer of 2006 gang affiliation and often unreported gang violence escalated in Red borough. This is evidenced by the shoot-out at a well-known shopping street in the summer of 2006 that involved half a dozen or so youths clad in bulletproof vests. The summer of 2006 also saw two fatal shootings, as the ownership of illicit firearms in the borough rose. For some young people involuntary gang affiliation can have dire consequences:

What is often ignored is that many of the young men in this predicament do not actively seek out gang affiliation or involvement in gun crime. Many are mortified by what they have done and what they feel they have had to do to survive. Christopher gave an account of how one young person he knew was affected:

They're crouched up in the corner crying because they brought the gun out to protect themselves and they've been challenged so they've pulled the trigger. They haven't wanted to pull the trigger ...

In reality, being unable to 'escape' from the neighbourhoods where these crimes are being enacted, they cannot afford to appear resistant or indifferent to the powerful groups and individuals who are involved. Moreover, gun ownership in a neighbourhood tends to become self-propelling, as those who feel threatened by other young people with firearms, arm themselves in self-defence. However, as a result of the historical legacy of mistrust, seeking help from the police is not an option. (Palmer and Pitts 2006)

3 Affiliation to gain access to educational/recreational resources in gang territory

Non-affiliation may mean that it is dangerous to use certain services or facilities, like an FE college or the local park, either located in gang territory or where access is only possible by traversing gang territory. The young person then has to decide whether to affiliate in order to take advantage of the resources that would be denied them by non-affiliation. In Red, White and Blue boroughs there were many gang-involved children and young people who were subject to few if any of the individual or familial risk factors said to be associated with gang membership. These young people were primarily interested in conventional activities – sport, music, art, etc. – but because of a paucity of youth provision, or its inaccessibility because it was in gang territory, they gravitated towards the gangs. However, because the 'centre of gravity' of these gangs is crime and violence, the young people associated with them were at heightened risk of both criminal involvement and criminal victimisation.

4 Affiliation because of lack of access to legitimate opportunity

For young people who fall out of education at an early age and have been in trouble with the law there are few acceptable, legitimate opportunities available to them. The problem is not simply that they lack the necessary skills, qualifications and personal credibility; it is also that in terms of their social class orientation and culturally shaped attitudes to the workplace, they are ill-equipped to survive in the few jobs available:

> ... foot dragging, attitudinal opposition, and petty theft. This kind of purposeful disgruntlement ... is particularly unacceptable in the new office service sector, where 'attitude' – enthusiasm, initiative, and flexibility – often determines who is fired and who is promoted. (Bourgois 1995)

In these circumstances, gang membership provides one of the few routes to a status-conferring role and a 'decent wage'.

5 Continued affiliation because of dangers inherent in leaving the gang

Gang members who want to leave the gang not only lose its protections, becoming vulnerable to other gangs with which they have previously had a beef; they may also fall foul of their former associates because of the disrespect or disloyalty implied by their departure. Derek in Red borough said:

> If I want to be out of the gang, I must leave this area. No way I could stay round here man. There is always someone to come after you with a blade or something.

While some young people wholeheartedly embrace and revel in gang membership, many of those interviewed in the course of this research appeared to be either ambivalent about, or resigned to gang membership, seeing few if any realistic alternatives.

6 Psychological dependence

As we note in Chapter 3, over time gang-affiliated young people, particularly if their bond to families and conventional institutions is tenuous, may develop a dependency upon the gang that will be reinforced by the threat posed by other gangs. It is these young people who are most likely to develop the distinctive beliefs and attitudes (Sampson and Lauritsen 1994; Kennedy 2007), behaviours (Short and Strodtbeck 1974; Pitts 2007b) mental health problems (Li *et al.* 2002) and crime patterns (Hagedorn 1998; Thornbury 1998) that set them apart.

Involuntary affiliation and the poverty of theory

In Chapter 3 we noted that in the criminal justice system criminality is explained in terms of the moral character, proclivities or deficiencies of criminal individuals. And this is reflected in the organisational structures and operational imperatives of criminal justice agencies, as well as the theories of criminal motivation employed by the criminologists, who service the system. As Michel Foucault (1972) has observed, because institutional power generates forms of knowledge about institutional subjects, the individualising imperative of the judicial system demarcates both the *problematique* (that which is to be explained) of criminology and popular discourses of criminality. Thus, in our time, the individualising imperative is evident in both popular and scholarly, mainstream and radical, accounts of gang formation.

However, these potted lay and social-scientific accounts of the origins of 'gang affiliation' all fail to recognise the power of the machinery of intimidation and coercion at work in gang-affected neighbourhoods, and the choices it necessitates for the young people confined there.

The risk factor paradigm holds that subjects exposed to 'criminogenic risk factors' develop erroneous cognitions, weakened bonds to conventional institutions and a diminished capacity for self-control. Gang affiliation is therefore a product of the social and psychological deficits of gang members and their families (cf. Farrington 2002).

Enchantment (c.f. the lyre of Orpheus) is a lay criminology that contends that subjects introject and enact attitudes and behaviours depicted in provocative musical sub-genres like 'gangsta rap'. Gang affiliation is therefore a product of enchantment wherein subjects are presented with an irresistible albeit bogus account of their predicament, a vocabulary of motives and techniques and a soundtrack to accompany the action.

Seduction (aka Cultural Criminology) has subjects drawn to the deviant enterprise because of its transgressive nature, 'the dialectic of fear and pleasure', and the liberation it offers from the mundane demands of conventional life (cf. Katz 1988). Gang affiliation is therefore a product of the indulgence of forbidden desires.

Cultural attrition is another lay criminology that holds that parental authority in ethnic minority households is undermined by culturally insensitive laws and policies that restrict the right of parents to inflict the degree of culturally prescribed physical chastisement sufficient to deter their children from gang affiliation. Gang affiliation is therefore a product of ethnocentric legal constraints upon parental autonomy.

Thwarted consumerism has subjects inducted into and enthralled by 'late modern' consumer culture, but denied the means to participate. They therefore resort to illicit means to fund their participation (cf. Fitzgerald *et al.* 2003; Hallsworth and Young 2004). Gang affiliation is therefore, a reaction to the subject's 'thwarted consumerism'.

Rational choice theory posits subjects who calculate their advantage in terms of the costs and benefits that will flow from any given socially deviant act (cf. Clarke 1983). Gang affiliation is therefore the product of rational calculation.

Routine activities theory maintains that local, situational and cultural factors legitimise/rationalise certain forms of social deviance within a particular geographical/social/cultural milieu (cf. Sutherland and Cressy 1966; Felson 1998). Gang affiliation is therefore a routine adaptation to local normative structures.

Status frustration holds that lower-class boys, disadvantaged by mainstream middle-class institutions, experience status frustration, producing a 'reaction formation' in which mainstream values are inverted and then enacted (cf. Cohen 1955). Gang affiliation is therefore a product of subconscious processes triggered by class/cultural conflict.

Social strain theory argues that lower-class young people, denied access to legitimate opportunity, band together to devise illegitimate means to achieve socially valorised material goals (cf. Cloward and Ohlin 1960). Gang affiliation is therefore an alternative route to opportunity. (Rather than the life-threatening termination of opportunity it becomes for some young people.)

The 'masculinity' thesis suggest that economically disadvantaged, and hence socially emasculated, lower-class young men find in the gang an arena in which to enact forms of hyper-masculinity that enable them to sustain a plausible male identity (cf. Newburn and Stanko 1995). Gang affiliation is, therefore, a product of socio-economically induced gender insecurity.

Signification holds that 'agents of social control' misrecognise relatively innocuous adolescent behaviour, imposing pejorative labels that spoil identity, causing subjects to adopt 'gangsta' as their 'master role', thus setting in train deviant careers (cf. Becker 1963; Cicourel 1968; Goffman 1968). Gang affiliation is therefore a product of the introjection of a negative stereotype as one's 'master role'.

The Risk factor paradigm, Enchantment, Thwarted consumerism, Seduction, Social strain, Routine activities, Status frustration and the *Masculinity thesis* understand gang affiliation as a product of an involuntary 'gravitation' and/or 'contagion' (Matza 1969). *Signification* understands gang affiliation as a product of ascription. *Rational choice* and *cultural attrition* understand it as essentially voluntaristic. What unites them is an assumption that however 'wrong-headed' the subject may be, they believe, or act as if, gang affiliation is a positive 'choice'. Nowhere in these accounts is there any notion that the actor may be constrained by fear or coercion to act in ways they would not have chosen. The masculinity thesis, for example, fails to address the threat posed to, and the fear induced in, young men by the caricatured hyper-masculinities enacted within gang culture and demanded of them as the price of admission, albeit a price that may be reluctantly paid.

Rational choice theory is usually understood as a process wherein individuals weigh the costs of apprehension and punishment against the potential pecuniary benefits of a criminal act. In this calculation there are only two actors, the individual and the state, with the state, as Max Weber (1947) observes, having a 'monopoly on the legitimate use of force' (*Gewaltmonopol des Staates*) to constrain and punish the wrongdoer.

For the reluctant gangster, however, costs and benefits are calculated first and foremost in terms of their personal safety and that of their family and friends, not the pecuniary benefits that might accrue to a criminal act. In this calculation there are three actors: the individual, the gang and the state. And while the state may theoretically retain a 'monopoly on the legitimate use of force', most residents in gangland perceive it as either unable or unwilling to use that force to protect them from the virtual monopoly on the illegitimate use of force enjoyed by the neighbourhood gang.

The idea of involuntary affiliation describes most accurately the bind in which increasing numbers of young people in the poorest neighbourhoods in Britain find themselves. It offers a more coherent explanation of their criminal motivation, and the evolution of their criminal careers in this dangerous world, awash with drugs, money and firearms, than the accounts offered by much contemporary criminology and the law.

The law, locked into the individualising, volitional, imperative, cannot easily deal with a world characterised by cultures of conflict, coercion and control and involuntary affiliation. Its solution, 'joint enterprise', is simple but effective; everybody becomes equally culpable. Following the northern 'riots', fermented by the British National Party in 2004, more than 100 Asian young people were jailed. Passing sentence, the judge, David Boulton, observed:

> Although some of the defendants played minor roles, it was the combination that fuelled a large-scale disturbance. To some extent, all are responsible for everything. It is wrong and misleading to look at what any one person did in isolation. (*Burnley Today*, 8 November 2004)

David, whose story opened this chapter, was present at the tail end of a violent incident because, he says, 'sometimes you just have to be there'. Although he arrived at the incident after the fighting had stopped, and despite the fact that he is 'of previous good character', with no prior criminal convictions, he is, at the time of writing, serving a custodial sentence in a Young Offender Institution for joint enterprise to commit violent disorder. Thus, despite its responsibility to defend the victims of injustice, the criminal justice system becomes just another brick in the wall that confines David and many other young people like him within gangland.

Chapter 8

Living in neo-liberal gangland

Do they think we choose to live like this?

Hayley, peer mentor, X-It Programme, Brixton (2008)

Yes, so far as the individual is concerned ... it may very well be true that character is destiny. And the other way round. But on the larger scale, destiny is demographics; and demographics is a monster.

Martin Amis, *House of Meetings* (2007)

Gang-affiliated young people and their families

In her book *Estates*, Lynsey Hanley (2007) writes:

A population that is constantly trying to move on because of bad conditions will never settle down and build the kind of community that is strong enough to withstand economic and social shocks. The two most corrosive effects of poor housing are apathy and transience – when an estate is populated almost entirely by people who are either stuck there for the duration, rather than actively wanting to stay, or who are only there for a few months. People have to want to stay in order that they can fight for the conditions they deserve.

The story of violent youth gangs in England is to a large extent the story of these housing estates, the ones that most residents would leave tomorrow if they could. The Americans call them ghettoes: abandoned places peopled by families swept aside by the inexorable onward march of 'market society' (Currie 1985).

This is not how the people living there describe their lives. Many experience the effects of the social and economic forces that bear upon them as personal failure, a source of shame and guilt. Others develop a profound indifference that extends to all areas of their lives. Some just become depressed. It is as if living where they do and as they do serves to call into question their competence as human beings, a sense compounded by the feeling that they cannot protect their children.

Several informants in Red and Blue boroughs said that communication between gang-involved young people and their families was often difficult, that parents frequently did not know where their children were and felt unable to exert control over them. For their part, some gang-involved young people felt that their parents were worn down by the circumstances of their lives and so they couldn't turn to them for support. A White borough social worker said:

> I think their parents are too stretched with trying just to make a living. They haven't got time to care.

For some families there may be a sense of disappointment and humiliation at the evaporation, or unrealisability, of the 'migrant's dream' of upward social mobility. Other parents may feel shame and frustration at being unable to extricate their families from this highly dangerous situation. These parents are all too aware of the widespread perception that the gang problem is ultimately a product of poor parenting and that the solution lies in assuming responsibility for their children. Yet most feel unable either to control or to protect their children. As a Red borough gang worker put it:

> Telling these families to take responsibility for their kids' behaviour is like telling them to take their kids into the jungle and take responsibility for them not getting eaten by lions and tigers.

In such circumstances parents must calculate whether their child's interest is best served by resisting the gang or affiliating with it. Some parents consequently appear to collude with their child's gang involvement because to be in the gang is the safest option. In these circumstances, a YOT worker observed:

... it is crucial not to blame parents for the gang phenomenon, they are doing what they can with minimal support in a highly dangerous and complex situation.

This has strong echoes of North American research, which found that gang-involved families require a high level of emotional support (Hagedorn 1998).

Political negligence

The last two decades have witnessed the 'secession of the successful', the economically and socially mobile from these gang-affected estates. Meanwhile, much-needed urban renewal schemes, by displacing established residents, thereby undermining their capacity to exert social control and offer social support, have inadvertently compounded the problem. This erosion of solidarity has served to produce a defensive individualism on these estates and undermined the capacity of residents to act collectively to effect political change (cf. Wilson 1987). Gwendoline, a resident on the Causeway estate in Red borough said:

As far as they are concerned we don't exist, and even if we do, we are just some kind of problem that won't go away. I sometimes think the best thing we could do would be to all get together and go out and vote and demand that our politicians listen to what's happening to us.

Like other residents, she bemoaned the absence of a political voice in the borough that would speak on behalf of the victimised neighbourhood.

This absence of political solidarity means that the political and material resources required to combat the gangs are not drawn down into the neediest neighbourhoods. The community group that is most effective in Red borough is Parents Against Violence, because it builds on the remnants of the social and political solidarity of an older generation of primarily African-Caribbean parents.

Gang-involved young people

The long-term prospects for core gang members are bleak. A gang worker in Red borough said:

They end up doing a long prison sentence, cracked-out or dead.

While young people on the margins of the gang may from time to time talk about the dangers of, and alternatives to, gang involvement, those more heavily involved appear to be 'in denial'. A social worker said:

They seem to have a kind of defence mechanism that prevents them thinking about the likely end point of their gang careers.

Several respondents in Red, White and Blue boroughs referred to this state of denial. A social worker in White borough observed that in gang members' families, the 'feeling', if it is done at all, is usually done by parents and siblings, some of whom may act as mediators between these emotionally 'switched-off' and potentially dangerous young people and their adversaries.

A psychotherapist working with gang-involved young people in east London described them as 'emotionally unavailable', and this suspension of feeling appears to be a key feature of what another adult respondent described as the 'gang mentality'. The nature of gang territoriality gives a clue to the 'militarised' mindset of the Younger/Soldier:

JP: *What happens when you go inside, do they put you with people from your own gang?*

Adrian: *Sort of, but it's different inside, it's north, south, east and west.*

JP: *How do you mean?*

Adrian: *Then it's east London boys against south London or west London. And then, if they transfer you to a nick up north, it's London against Manchester or Liverpool. You know what I mean?*

JP: *Supposing you made friends inside with someone from another gang or another area, what would happen when you came out?*

Adrian: *Same as before, we'd both know that, that's just how it is.*

Such ardent hierarchical affiliation to the gang, the area and the city is reminiscent of other more conventional commitments to, for example, football teams. But in the case of football, for the most part at least, the conflict is symbolic and for the majority affiliation to a football club does not preclude emotional closeness to other people in the way that gang affiliation appears to. And it may be that in the dangerous world inhabited by gang members, this passionate but disembodied relationship with a place serves to suppress the anxiety and despair that the realistic prospect of the loss of one's own life or that of a close friend or relative might otherwise induce.

The impact on neighbourhoods

Gang involvement may change over time but the affiliation to and affection for territory – 'my neighbourhood', 'my area', 'my estate' – appears to remain constant. But this territory must be protected from outsiders, leading one young respondent to say that he would defend anyone who lived in his postcode.

This commitment to the defence of territory appears to have its origins in the constraints imposed by the geography of the drugs market. However, increasingly, territory is defined as a postcode, and the antagonisms generated are London-wide, bearing little if any relation to drug markets or gang territories. The territorial violence and aggression at this level appears to serve little practical purpose beyond providing an arena in which individuals and groups can demonstrate their physical prowess and courage; to that extent it has resonances with football violence in its heyday. However, the arbitrariness and ferocity of this violence also has strong echoes of the conflicts between Yardie groups in Jamaica and in the UK.

One of the more sinister aspects of gang culture in the three boroughs is the apparent determination of some gangs to exert control over the other residents in the territories they claim as their own. A youth worker in White borough named three housing estates that had to all intents and purposes become no-go areas for non-residents, and to that extent they were coming to resemble the garrison communites of Kingston, Jamaica described by Gunst (2003).

What is distinctive about the garrison communities of Kingston is not merely that gang members live there and defend them from other gangs. Nor is it that they are also drugs markets. It is that the gangs exert inordinate control over the day-to-day lives of other residents. As we have seen, in some neighbourhoods where gangs operate, unaffiliated young people and adults have been subject to intimidation, harassment, theft, violent assault and rape. In controlling the day-to-day behaviour of residents and tenants living within 'their' territory, controlling who may enter 'their' territory and driving out those who they believe should not dwell there, some gangs are transforming the estates where they live into the 'totalitarian social space(s) in which the options of the residents are largely controlled', described by Figueroa and Sives (2002) in their discussion of the 'garrison communities'. The capacity of gangs to instil fear and thereby silence would-be complainants and witnesses appears to free the Youngers to commit offences with impunity. A Red borough housing officer said:

> For five or six years a group of 16 to 18-year-olds was terrorising Auden and Isherwood Towers. They would wait at the bottom of the lift and take money, mobile phones, clothes that they fancied, even a dog, from the residents. A younger sister also had these terrible parties in the foyer but nobody complained. The police had been trying to prosecute for years but because of witness intimidation residents stayed quiet. These kids came to believe they were untouchable. Eventually we achieved an ASBO and a committal to Court, which resulted in a prison sentence, but the residents needed enormous support from the police and ourselves.

A Red borough Better Neighbourhoods officer said:

> The Cummings estate is a neutral space and neutral spaces are colonised by gangs because nothing and nobody seems to be able to stop them. So neutral territory becomes gang territory by default. Since the summer, the gang from the Lowry estate, some of them as young as 12, meet here before they go down to the Causeway estate. They intimidate the local children and young people. They put messages on MySpace saying 'we are coming to get you'. They beat them up on the way back from school and they even try to break into their houses to get at them.

This raises the question of whether this apparent desire on the part of gang members to dominate the lives of those around them flows from the erosion of informal social control and its effects on certain poorly socialised individuals or, more ominously, whether it has become a defining characteristic of youth gang culture in some neighbourhoods.

Surveys suggest that a majority of tenants on gang-affected estates would move if they could. However, all the London boroughs have long housing waiting lists and this, together with the transfer of housing responsibility to a plurality of housing associations, makes it difficult for them to move within, or out of, particular boroughs. Those who are successful have usually negotiated a house-swap, but this is difficult if they live on an estate with a reputation for gang violence. Some tenants have been moved to the north of England where social housing is more plentiful. However, few are willing to countenance such a radical solution.

Although a great deal of money has been invested in regeneration, and the new homes are of a high standard, many tenants continue to suffer from low incomes and unemployment.

Residents and tenants, particularly if they live alone, do not come together to find solutions, and are more likely to take their problems to the housing authorities. However, when a housing authority endeavours to formalise complaints, which requires a named complainant and/or witnesses, most of these complaints evaporate.

But even when a housing association, in desperation, applies for an ASBO, this cumbersome process can take up to two years, by which time its significance for the complainant and its impact on the perpetrator will have dissipated. The difficulties surrounding the imposition of civil or criminal sanctions means that many people on gang-affected estates come to believe that nobody is interested in their plight. And so they stop complaining and simply lock their doors. As a result, the gang-involved young people on the estate come to believe that they are untouchable.

On the Causeway estate in Red borough in 2006, where the 'climate of fear' was said to be most intense, the leader of the Tenants and Residents Association (TRA) tried to stand up to the gangs, but the threat to his safety and that of his family was such that the housing authority and the police persuaded him to move house.

More recently, according to the Chair of another TRA in Red borough, police Safer Neighbourhood Teams have been effective in encouraging people to express their concerns:

When they see the police around constantly they think things are changing.

However, some housing professionals point to a mismatch between available resources, particularly youth provision and policing, on gang-affected estates. This is, they argue, determined by the political clout of particular TRAs, and the extent to which the different housing providers see their responsibility extending beyond the maintenance of the fabric of their properties.

The impact on schools

In some primary schools in the three boroughs, some children were claiming to be gang members, and gang-based fights had occurred in the playground. Some respondents said that 'Tinys' were carrying knives and drugs for older gang members. Mobile phones meant that gang-related fights that started in primary schools quickly attracted gang-involved students from secondary schools, and some primary schools had a regular police presence at the end of the school day.

Pressures towards involvement in gangs are heightened in schools with high levels of bullying and violence. In Blue borough, youth workers said that schools were 'coded' as gang territory, and gang-related conflict at the end of the school day and on the bus journey to and from school was not uncommon. In Red borough, some schools with high levels of gang-related conflict tended to serve areas of acute social deprivation with high levels of transience and this meant that the student 'pecking order' was never settled and conflict was continual The turmoil was exacerbated by technology; mobile phones and texting brought gang-related tensions into schools, so that there was no respite from rumours, threats and the attendant disruption. This meant that in some schools, teachers were more or less powerless to shape the learning environment and attainment levels suffered accordingly. Some teachers in gang-affected schools described themselves as a 'thin blue line', finding it difficult to 'stay motivated'. Such an environment is, of course, inimical to academic achievement. Taken together, these factors meant that gang-involved and gang-affected children and young people were educationally disadvantaged, sometimes profoundly so, and this in turn disadvantaged them in the labour market.

Some secondary schools had developed strategies for minimising the impact of gangs inside school, including:

- Meeting students at the school gates every day.
- Banning bandanas and other gang paraphernalia.
- Cleaning off gang-related graffiti as soon as it appeared.
- Developing intensive mentoring, for gang-involved or gang-affected students.
- Addressing questions of gangs, guns, drugs and violence in Citizenship and PSHE classes.
- Consistently challenging street culture and its attendant attitudes and behaviours.

Inside these schools there is actually little evidence of overt gang conflict. The head of a secondary school that draws students from two rival gang-affected estates in Red borough said:

I think the children are relieved to leave gang culture outside. We have a zero tolerance policy on knives. We use security wands and conduct random searches; we agreed this with the parents. We have rules: no hoods, no hats, no caps and no bandanas. We say to them that the street stays on the street.

She argued that in this way the children are given the option of embracing school values rather than street values because they feel safe inside the school. This allows them to drop the posture and so they are freed from their dilemma about gang loyalty. A young respondent at this school, a gang member, echoed this:

In schools everyone is friendly – you grow up together from years 3 and 4.

Teachers said that students will sometimes talk to staff about some of the things that happen on the estates where they live, but will often say, 'I can't tell you what's going on out there.' Outside school many students feel that they are physically under threat and they are fearful for themselves and their families. A teacher in White borough said:

They live in the middle of it and cannot see a way out of it.

A recently arrived student at a secondary school in Red borough was badly beaten up by rival gang members on his way to school. However, suggestions by staff that they should call the police were met with horror. He said:

If they think I did that we [my family] will have to leave the country. We have already moved once because of threats from gangs.

Similarly, a boy with no gang involvement who had inadvertently witnessed a gang shooting involving a gang-affiliated schoolmate had to be transferred to another school because even a slight suspicion that he would 'talk' would have put him and his family in danger.

Schools and their students can become the target of gang crime. In late 2006, a group of Youngers from a local gang targeted year 11s at a secondary school in Red borough for one week, at lunchtimes, taking mobile phones and cash from them. At one point a gang member, who was apparently 'cracked out', came into the school and started smashing up its foyer. When a visiting mother objected, the boy pulled a gun on her and demanded her phone. A very brave member of staff intervened and talked the boy out of the building. The boy was arrested on unrelated charges the following week.

In one secondary school in White borough, staff expressed concern that several of their year 9 and 10 girls (ages 13–14) were being exploited by considerably older gang-involved men. This abuse of vulnerable young women appeared to be commonplace in gangland. A teacher in Red borough said:

One of my year 10 students was recently gang-raped by some gang members. I talked to her and her mother. They are obviously very frightened and the mother insists that it was consensual. The girl won't come to counselling because she is afraid of being seen to talk to anyone in authority about it.

Secondary school staff expressed concern that children from violent, sometimes gang-involved, families tended to reproduce this violence in school. They were also worried that some parents, faced with the threat posed to their children, and themselves, by gangs, guns and drugs, and unable to do anything about it, appeared to have entered a state of denial.

Increased gang activity in and around primary and secondary schools in the early years of the twenty-first century had led to higher rates of exclusion, and several schools in Red borough cited 'gangs' as the reason for missed targets in their Ofsted self-assessments. Many of these exclusions arose from young people bringing weapons into school, an infraction that triggers automatic exclusion in most schools. But, of course, it is often the fear generated by gangs that induces non-gang-affiliated young people to bring weapons into school.

In the past, schools have been loath to go public about gang problems for fear of jeopardising their year 7 intake. However, in Red borough staff believed that the education authority was now viewing the problem as one that belonged to the education authority rather than a particular school or school head. At a practical level, this meant that non-gang-affected schools were becoming more willing to lend a hand with the placement of school-excluded gang-involved children and young people.

The impact on further education colleges

Respondents in all three boroughs suggested that further education colleges were often contested gang territory. Gang members in Red borough told us that unlike schools, further education colleges 'belong to' particular gangs. Indeed, in Red borough in September 2006, new students attending an ICT course at one college reported that they were being warned off by gang members claiming ownership. While this ownership does not appear to impinge upon non-gang-involved students, there have been several incidents of gang violence. In one Red borough college two members of Cromwell Close were said to have been stabbed by members of Cruise, and in 2005 a boy believed to have been stabbed in an FE college stumbled bleeding into the toilet block of his old secondary school to use the washing facilities. Although these could be isolated incidents and the young informants could be exaggerating, several professionals suggested that gang activity in FE colleges in the borough was gaining momentum.

The impact on youth work

Over the past two decades, youth work in all three boroughs has been seriously depleted by cutbacks (Crimmens *et al.* 2004). Most youth workers we spoke to felt that they were only able to make a limited response to a growing problem. Outreach workers in Red borough see gang-based 'territorialism' as a major problem for youth work. They argue that gang territories and gang pressures shape what can be done, where it can be done and with whom. A team working on an estate in the south of Red borough to develop recreational opportunities for local children and young people saw their work confounded by the Youngers from a nearby estate-based gang who intimidated the young people to the point that they dared not engage in those activities. This also poses a real physical threat to the workers. A youth worker in White borough said:

I don't think youth workers should be going onto these estates alone and I think in some places we should be issuing flak jackets – I'm very serious about this.

A youth worker in Red borough said:

I think the danger is that social strategies could be paralysed by territorialism. This is happening in schools and colleges and if it continues we could see the gangs effectively paralysing public services.

Moreover, because the bulk of statutory youth service provision is building-based, its availability, or not, will be determined by the gang territory into which it falls.

Workers in Red borough said that group work with gangs is very difficult and may even be counter-productive (cf. Klein 1969), suggesting that effective intervention with core gang members may need to be done on a one-to-one basis, as is the case in Prolific and Priority Offenders programmes (cf. Marlow 2007).

Much of the youth work and play provision in Red borough is funded by housing associations. However, this means that the volume and nature of provision is determined by the housing association's understanding of its role *vis-à-vis* young people living in social housing. Housing providers vary considerably in their responsiveness to residents' social needs. A housing professional said:

For some, housing associations' 'guardianship' means first and foremost a focus on the fabric of the buildings rather than the anxieties of tenants and residents. For many housing associations, engagement with gang issues would be a major 'step beyond'.

As a result, youth provision is very patchy. But even when the housing provider does make provision for young people, 'territorialism' means that nobody outside the area demarcated by the gang is able to use that provision.

Residents and professionals see a need for structured opportunities for the various youth work providers to talk to one another, to the voluntary sector youth services, to housing providers, the police, the YOT and tenants and residents, about the impact of gangs on youth provision in the borough. Alongside this, they say, there should be a discussion with the young people on their estates about their social and recreational needs and what would constitute 'cool' provision. Ultimately, they argue, there has to be a shared youth strategy that articulates with those of the other agencies endeavouring to confront the gang problem in the borough.

The impact on the Youth Offending Team

In a caseload survey in Red borough, we found that over 40 per cent of the young people supervised by the Youth Offending Team (YOT) were gang involved, and this is probably an underestimate because the more heavily involved young people are the less likely they are to admit it. One of the issues facing the YOT is that because of problems of territoriality young people involved in group work have to be bussed in to the premises to avoid crossing, or passing through, territory claimed by rival gangs. This is also a problem in White and Blue boroughs.

Policing gangland

The pessimism and political quiescence of gang-affected families is compounded by the belief that the police are powerless to provide, and may be uninterested in providing, adequate protection from gang violence.

Among black respondents we found a profound ambivalence about whether Operation Trident, which targets gun crime in the black community, constitutes a benefit, because all too often, they say, it appears to ignore the complexities of knife and gun ownership and armed conflict, and fails to distinguish between the instigators of gang violence and those children and young people drawn unwillingly into gang involvement.

Policing is shaped by nationally determined targets, changing political priorities and local need. However, there are tensions between national priorities, and the targets and penalties that accompany them, and the complexities of local law enforcement.

Police officers in Red borough, interviewed in 2004, attributed the low priority accorded to the burgeoning gang-related crack cocaine problem in the borough to the national emphasis on tackling street crime (Red Borough Crime Disorder and Drugs Audit 2004). Red borough was one of 15 local authorities chosen as a pilot area for intensive action against street crime in 2002–03 and one of three chosen in 2003–04. Today, street crime remains a priority, but since 2006 terrorism has been the number one policing issue in the borough, and significant resources have been committed to this work.

This dual emphasis upon terrorism and street crime, both real and pressing problems, has tended to deflect police time and resources from the problem of armed, crack-dealing youth gangs, and in consequence the borough's police have yet to attract the kinds of resources that the dimensions of the problem would appear to merit. This is somewhat ironic since street crime, particularly where it is gun-enabled, drug-dealing and drug use, as well as much sexual offending, anti-social behaviour and fear of crime in the borough appear to be inextricably tied up with gang activity.

The police recognise that the 'gang problem' requires a long-term, 'joined-up' strategy involving high-level, multi-agency strategic leadership. However, it is in the nature of contemporary public services that they tend to be driven by short- or medium-term imperatives. Moreover, because senior police officers are employed on time-limited contracts and evaluated against ever-changing, nationally determined performance indicators, there are 'perverse incentives' within the system to steer policing away from long-term strategic thinking about local problems.

National priorities and demands upon resources mean that police gang strategies have to be fairly tightly focused, aiming to 'take out' the top tier in each gang and where possible to seize their assets. In doing this the police draw upon evidence about gang-involved groups and individuals generated by Source Units. However, by removing an entire echelon of a gang, the way is cleared for an internal struggle for leadership and an external struggle for market domination, both of which can generate armed violence. A further consequence of 'taking out' the Elders is that younger, more volatile and hence more dangerous people are left in charge, without the 'restraining hand' (*sic*) of the Elders. Moreover, the eventual return of the Elders from prison can spark further violence as they endeavour to take back control of the gang and avenge the 'disrespect' they may have endured during their time inside.

Clearly, the job of the police is to catch people who commit serious crime, but without a parallel intervention that aims to avert some of the unintended consequences of successful police action, this strategy does not contribute as much as it might to the safety and security of residents in gang-affected neighbourhoods. This raises the question of what the police should be doing with these gangs between these periodic 'busts'. One Red borough police officer, who has made a point of maintaining close contact with senior gang members, stressed the importance of a high-profile police presence in gang neighbourhoods:

They need to know you and to know that you know them and what they are up to. I think some police officers are reluctant to get involved at that level but otherwise these guys come to believe they are living charmed lives and can get away with anything. They need to know we are there.

The establishment in 2007 of Safer Neighbourhoods Teams (SNT) in Red borough appears to be moving some way towards this, and it is obviously encouraging some previously reluctant residents to come forward with their concerns about gangs. However, their success relies on the development of trust, which can be undermined by discontinuity and the absence of the interpersonal skills needed to engage with a frightened and distrustful public. A local resident said:

For the first year it [the SNT] was excellent. But then the sergeant who knew everybody left. Then they went down to one PC and one PCSO and it kind of fell apart. You need to see them more. There's a new sergeant now and he's really efficient but he's still got to develop the same people skills to win the trust and confidence of local people if it's going to work.

There is a long history of resistance to a police presence in London schools. Currently there are eight officers placed in Red borough schools and the police would like to have a presence in all gang-affected schools. Relationships between the police and schools appear to be improving and requests for advice about knife arches and security wands are increasing.

The robbery squad in Red borough adopted a strategy of seeking ASBOs on younger repeat offenders who have previously avoided arrest and prosecution by intimidating witnesses. Because it requires a lower standard of proof and carries a criminal sanction the police believe that ASBOs may be an effective weapon against this type of street crime.

The police are concerned that the criminal justice system often fails to understand the dynamics of the gang problem. Recently two trials, one involving the Causeway Gang and the other their arch-enemy Cromwell Close, were scheduled in the same court on the same day. On spotting this, protagonists from both sides phoned for reinforcements, in the form of firearms, which were fortuitously intercepted by two observant police officers patrolling outside the court, thus averting a bloodbath.

The police are also frustrated by the fact that because the Crown Prosecution Service (CPS) is overly target-driven prosecutors tend to 'play the odds', only supporting prosecutions that have a very strong chance of success. The police find this approach unsupportive, arguing that if they are to send the right message to gangs, the CPS must become less risk-averse. They argue that public protection relies on the certainty that if someone intimidates complainants or witnesses they will be prosecuted.

How many people are adversely affected by gangs?

It is difficult to calculate accurately how many people are adversely affected by gangs. In the 2001 census, Red borough had a population of around 250,000, of which 30 per cent (around 75,000 people) fell within the 10–29 age group. We estimate that around 375 young people are directly involved in gangs, representing 0.5 per cent of the age group. We also estimate that a further 0.5 per cent are directly adversely affected by gangs and that a further 2 per cent are indirectly adversely affected, because they live in an area or attend a school where gang activity threatens them or limits what they are able to do. If this is so, gangs adversely affect the day-to-day lives of around 2.5 per cent, or 1,875, children and young people in the borough in the 10–29 age group. But these young people also have parents and siblings who are affected by their predicament. We estimate their number to be around 4,000. Thus, in the region of 6,000 people in Red borough (approximately 2.5 per cent of the total population) would appear to be adversely affected by youth gangs. This calculation does not include the professionals directly and indirectly involved with and affected by gangs.

Chapter 9

If every child mattered

Everybody on the street knows they're going to lose; it's just that we don't know how to win.

Gang worker, Red borough

Don't agonise; organise.

Saul Alinsky, Rules for Radicals (1971)

The analysis developed in the foregoing chapters suggests that inasmuch as we must intervene, here and now, to limit the damage wrought by violent youth gangs, in doing so we also need to lay the foundations for a longer-term strategy; one that stems the flow of young people entering gangland.

Here and now: gang suppression initiatives

One clear message from attempts to suppress gang violence is that suppression alone will not do it. The other is that whatever we do, we must do in a partnership between central and local government, public services, the voluntary sector and the children, young people and families who live in gang-affected neighbourhoods.

One of the most coherent and best-evaluated US gang interventions in recent years has been the Comprehensive Gang Strategy developed by the US Department of Justice Office of Juvenile Justice and Delinquency Prevention (OJJDP) in the 1990s. The strategy is based on the assumption that gangs become a chronic problem in communities where key organisations are inadequately integrated and insufficient resources are available to target gang-involved young people. The model identifies five key strategies that communities should incorporate into their programmes (see Figure 9.1).

In 1994 OJJDP launched demonstration projects in five US cities. One of the larger programmes, the Little Village Gang Violence Reduction Project in Chicago (Spergel and Grossman 1997), compared outcomes for 195 'program youths', 90 'quasi-program youths', who

---

1 *Community mobilisation.* Local citizens and organisations are involved in a common enterprise. The programme consists of local police officers, probation officers, community youth workers, church groups, boys' and girls' clubs, community organisations, and local residents working as a team to understand the gang structures and provide social intervention and social opportunities whenever they can.

2 *Social intervention.* The programme reaches out to youths unable to connect with legitimate social institutions. The youth, the gang structure, and the environmental resources must be taken into account before the youth is provided with crisis counselling, family counselling, or referral to services such as drug treatment, jobs, training, educational programmes, or recreation.

3 *Provision of social opportunities.* Youths at different points in their lives need different things. Older gang members may be ready to enter the legitimate job field and need training and education to do so. Younger youths at risk of becoming gang members may need alternative schools or family counselling. The programme should provide individualised services for each youth based on his or her needs.

4 *Suppression.* This not only consists of surveillance, arrest, probation and imprisonment to stop violent behaviour but also involves good communication between agency service providers and control providers. All providers jointly decide what happens to a particular youth when trouble arises or when it is about to.

5 *Organisational change and the development of local agencies and groups.* All workers need to work closely with one another and collaborate. Former gang members working as community youth workers need to be given as much respect as the police officers in the programme. Each group can provide important information for the programme that the other may not be able to obtain.

Figure 9.1 The comprehensive gang model

received some services, and 208 youths who received no services. The researchers concluded that a co-ordinated project approach, using a combination of social intervention and suppression, was more effective with more violent young people, whereas youth work alone was more effective with less violent youngsters. The programme was most effective in assisting older adolescents and young adults to reduce their criminal activities (particularly violence) more quickly than if no project services had been provided. Residents in target areas reported a greater sense of safety, a significantly reduced gang influence and increased police effectiveness.

In three OJJDP demonstration sites, however, there was no significant change in arrest patterns, which Spergel and Grossman (1997) attribute to 'poor program implementation'. These communities had difficulty establishing successful inter-agency collaboration and tended to neglect one or more of the five specified programme elements.

The OJJDP model, with its emphasis on inter-agency collaboration, community involvement and social intervention with gang members, was a key point of reference in the development of Operation Ceasefire, the influential strategy devised by the Boston Police Gang Unit, a modified version of which, the Manchester Multi-Agency Gang Strategy (MMAGS, see Figure 9.2 p. 130) has been developed in Manchester (UK) (Bullock and Tilley 2003). Following the implementation of Operation Ceasefire in mid 1996, a rigorous analysis was conducted by the John F. Kennedy School of Government at Harvard University (Braga *et al.* 2001). It concluded that the programme had been responsible for a fall in youth homicides in Boston from an average of 44 per year between 1991 and 1995 to 26 in 1996 and 15 in 1997, a trend that continued through 1998 and 1999.

The objective of Operation Ceasefire is simple. It aims to save lives and reduce serious injury. The Boston strategy had three elements:

1 *Co-ordinated leverage on gangs.* In gang-affected neighbourhoods, certain proscribed behaviours, like possession or use of knives and firearms, harassment and serious assaults, would trigger highly publicised multi-agency crackdowns by organisations with enforcement responsibilities. In the UK these enforcement agencies could be the:

• Police
• Probation service

- Youth Justice Service
- Housing authorities
- Social Services departments
- Environmental Health
- Trading Standards
- Educational Welfare Service
- DVLA
- TV Licensing Authority
- Benefits Agency
- Crown Prosecution Service
- Courts

The Boston strategy assumes that if the efforts of all or most enforcement agencies can be brought to bear simultaneously on groups and individuals suspected of, or perpetrating, proscribed behaviours, this will serve as a powerful disincentive. Co-ordinated leverage does not aim to 'smash' gangs but to alter the behaviour of gang-involved young people. For this strategy to be effective, publicity is crucial. Gang members are told in person by the police and youth workers that a crackdown is occurring, leaflets are distributed and the media is briefed. One of the other objectives of co-ordinated leverage is to create a 'firebreak', a cessation of tit-for-tat conflict whereby the need to carry weapons for self-defence is obviated.

As originally conceived, the Boston strategy appears to be based upon the assumption that certain families and communities are colluding with, or giving ambiguous messages to their children about involvement in gangs. However, the evidence from Red, White and Blue boroughs suggests that in many cases what may appear to be collusion is in fact a product of fear, intimidation and desperation. For such a strategy to be effective, therefore, only known or suspected perpetrators, not their families, nor their neighbours, should be targeted, since any perception of injustice, 'victim-blaming' or stereotyping would discredit the strategy, inducing resistance rather than the co-operation the strategy is designed to foster.

2 *Enhancing community relations.* This arm of the strategy aims to elicit local support for targeted crackdowns and develop the community's capacity to exert informal social control. However, in gang-affected neighbourhoods there is usually a high level of scepticism about and a mistrust of official intervention. Yet, as we have seen, in Red borough the advent of Safer Neighbourhood Teams has gone some way to countering this scepticism. Nonetheless,

Launched in 2001, by a partnership of the police, the probation service, the youth offending service, the education authority, housing, social services and the youth service, the Manchester Multi-Agency Gang Strategy (MMAGS) consists of a group of full-time staff seconded from the police, youth service, education and probation who offer diversionary educational, recreational and vocational activities to young people in or on the fringes of youth gangs. They work with up to 75 individuals, mostly aged between 10 and 25 at any one time. The project is voluntary; however, some youngsters are required to co-operate with MMAGS as a condition of a court order or licence. The project also runs sessions in schools and youth centres on issues such as gang culture, firearms legislation and peer pressure.

MMAGS makes contact with young people through:

- Referrals from partner agencies.
- Referrals from other agencies.
- Outreach by detached youth workers in gang-affected areas.
- Youth liaison officers who co-ordinate school/club programmes.
- Self-referral/direct contact with young people.

When a young person enters the programme the team undertakes an initial assessment with them to ascertain the type of diversionary programme that will meet their needs and gain their interest. The ensuing Intervention Action Plan (IAP) might involve several agencies (e.g. schools, social services, housing and the probation service) working together to deliver the programme components.

MMAGS preventive interventions also encompass:

- Detached youth work with young people.
- Sessions on gang issues as part of police crime days, which present the realities of life in a gang and alternatives to it.
- Work with local businesses to develop job opportunities.

MMAGS is funded by a combination of Neighbourhood Renewal, Building Safer Communities and Police Basic Command Unit grants. Seconded workers are half-funded by their agency. The total cost of running MMAGS is around £400,000 annually.

Although MMAGS is a statutory agency, it has an Independent Advisory Group composed of community members, and meets regularly with Mothers Against Violence, CARISMA, Victim Support and several other local voluntary sector organisations

In its first 12 months of operation MMAGS made contact with over 200 young people. It reintroduced several of these to education, with some gaining NVQ in motor mechanics. During this time, only 10 per cent of its 'target list' reoffended, suggesting that those who engage with MMAGS are more likely to renounce gang criminality.

Figure 9.2 The Manchester Multi-Agency Gang Strategy (MMAGS)

restoring trust in 'the authorities' and their capacity to take care of local people will be a long-term endeavour. William Julius Wilson (1987) has shown that one of the effects of social fragmentation in the poorest neighbourhoods is to undermine residents' capacity to act collectively to draw down much-needed resources. In Boston, police officers were often instrumental in galvanising public services into action and developing social, sporting and recreational provision in the neighbourhood. This had the important side-effect of generating support for the crackdowns on proscribed behaviours.

For the police in Boston, a longer-term objective was to garner the types of information from the community that would allow them to develop tightly targeted, intelligence-led interventions. But for this to happen, residents must feel that the authorities can offer them sufficient protection for as long as the threat persists. Thus, good community relations are ultimately predicated on the sustainability of police involvement in such an initiative.

3 *Engagement with gang members.* In Boston, social workers and youth workers utilised outreach methods to make contact with gang members on the street and offer them programmes that targeted their needs and created viable routes out of gang membership. These workers were quite explicit that their efforts were part and parcel of the 'crackdown'.

Malcolm Klein (1969) has famously warned against attaching street-based youth workers or social workers to particular gangs because of the danger of consolidating gang identity. However, as James Short and Fred Strodtbeck (1974) have pointed out, detached youth work is not synonymous with gang work and detached youth work remains one of the few means whereby we are able to make contact with hard-to-reach young people (see Crimmens *et al.* 2004).

In Manchester three additional elements were added to the Operation Ceasefire model:

1 *An inter-gang mediation service.* This aims to address long-standing rivalries and emerging tensions that cause shootings. While professionally based gang mediation services exist in the UK, the bulk of this work is undertaken by local organisations of parents and siblings of gang-involved young people, the clergy or professionals, like teachers, youth workers and certain police officers with close ties to the affected communities.

2 *Targeted protection/containment for victims.* For victims and repeat victims, because those who survive such attacks may retaliate or be victimised again. In the USA, interventions that support victims in finding alternative housing and relevant employment outside the area have proved effective in de-escalating gun crime, and 'safe houses' and relocation have become a feature of several anti-gang initiatives in the UK.

3 *Sensitisation of agencies.* This involves making all relevant agencies and organisations aware of the conditions that foster violent youth gangs, the far-reaching effects of gangs and the agencies responsibilities under Section 17 (Community Safety) of the Crime and Disorder Act (1998).

MMAGS results so far suggest that effective multi-agency gang strategies have the following characteristics:

- They draw upon, or establish links with, existing Crime and Disorder Partnerships.

- Their approach is rooted in a thorough and up-to-date analysis of the problem.

- They adopt a problem-solving approach, which is subject to regular review and revision in the light of fresh intelligence.

- They devise a clear plan and prioritisation of the elements of the problem(s) to be targeted, the requisite levels of intervention, the personnel who should intervene, the techniques and strategies they should adopt and the outcomes they will endeavour to achieve.

- They establish systems for collecting and sharing information and intelligence between all partners.

- They build strong links and create regular opportunities for contact with gang-affected populations in order to gain their support for the strategy.

- They encourage partners to review current practice in order to identify those elements that might be contributing to the problem rather than its resolution.

- They employ workers who are able to work in non-traditional ways, who identify with the young people being targeted and who are not intimidated by them. (But this can be a risky business.)

If, however, the violent youth gang problem is ever to be solved, these short- and medium-term interventions must be augmented by a longer-term strategy that reconnects beleaguered gang-affected neighbourhoods, families and children to the social, economic, vocational and cultural mainstream.

Stemming the flow

The *Every Child Matters* White Paper, published in 2004 and followed swiftly by the 2004 Children Act marked what the British government described as a 'new approach to the well-being of children and young people from birth to age 19'. The government's aim is that every child, whatever their background or circumstances, should have the support they need to:

- Be healthy.
- Stay safe.
- Enjoy and achieve.
- Make a positive contribution.
- Achieve economic well-being.

Were these aspirations to be realised, the gang problem would to all intents and purposes be solved. But if, as we have suggested, the progressive estrangement of gang-affected neighbourhoods from the socio-economic and cultural mainstream is at the heart of the youth gang problem, the response will have to go beyond the establishment of a national child protection database, the reorganisation of the existing under-resourced children's services into Children's Trusts and the all too familiar deployment of narrowly focused, short-term programmes or 'packages' designed to counteract proscribed beliefs, attitudes and behaviours among 'at risk' groups of children and young people (Bateman and Pitts 2005).

Whereas in the heyday of the welfare state governments endeavoured to ameliorate the depredations of the market by direct social and economic intervention, from the late 1970s policy has been progressively refocused upon equipping citizens for survival in an ever more turbulent global marketplace. This changed emphasis is part of a broader reconfiguration of the welfare state, wherein social policy is designed to buttress rather than burden the wealth producing economy (Taylor-Gooby 2003). In this shift from the 'welfare state' of old to a new 'social investment state' (Fawcett *et al.* 2004), the eradication of dependency and the promotion of future employability has become a central rationale for state expenditure upon children and young people.

Thus, investment in programmes of pre-school social education, teenage pregnancy reduction and social crime prevention is justified on the grounds that if the beliefs, attitudes and behaviours of these 'at risk' groups can be corrected, it will not only obviate the future costs of school failure, welfare dependency and crime, but also foster employability. This is why, across the sector in education, training, youth work, youth crime prevention and youth justice, we see such a heavy emphasis upon the eradication of supposedly self-defeating behaviours and attitudes; upon understanding the consequences of one's actions for oneself and others and the acquisition and accreditation of the life, social, educational and vocational skills that will, it is argued, facilitate a successful transition to the labour market. However, the realisation of the objectives of *Every Child Matters* in gang-affected neighbourhoods will require a great deal more than this.

Avoiding managerialism

Moreover, if these initiatives are to arise organically out of a dialogue between committed politicians, professionals and local citizens, young and old, as the evidence suggests they must, they should from the outset resist the blandishments of that modern-day enemy of promise, the 'new public management'. Most assessments of the impact of 'managerialism' in policing, children's services and youth justice have concluded that the perverse incentives intrinsic to the managerialist project have created a formidable barrier to the development of effective policy and practice (Cooper and Lousada 2005; Bateman and Pitts 2005; Hallam 2008). In youth justice, for example, the early promise of the multi-agency, multi-professional Youth Offending Team has been subverted by the Youth Justice Board's inordinate emphasis upon the achievement of specious and manipulable targets and the administration of demonstrably ineffective but quantifiable 'offending programmes' (Burnett and Appleton 2004; Bateman and Pitts 2005; Pitts 2007a). No; if we are to stem the flow, something else is needed, something more human, a response that feels as well as thinks, but when it thinks, thinks intelligently (Cooper and Lousada 2005).

A layered response

We now turn to a discussion of the components of medium- to long-term strategies to stem the flow of young people becoming involved in violent gang crime. Some of the initiatives cited have been or are being developed in Red, White and Blue boroughs, while others come from further afield. It is important to emphasise, however, that this is no *à la carte* menu, nor yet another dubious 'toolkit'. Rather it is a description of approaches and ideas that might inform a layered, integrated, response to the social, economic and cultural crisis that underlies the violent youth gang phenomenon in Britain.

The 'Anderlecht Initiative' offers a useful example of such a layered response. Anderlecht is a working-class neighbourhood close to the centre of Brussels where, until recently, low-paid manual and service-sector employment was relatively plentiful and housing was relatively cheap. As a result, the last few decades have seen an influx of poor overseas migrants, initially from the Maghreb but latterly from southern and eastern Europe. Mirroring the experience of many poor ethnic and cultural minority groups elsewhere in Europe, the young people in these communities tend to drop out of school earlier, obtain fewer qualifications, suffer significantly higher levels of unemployment and are more likely to be involved with the criminal justice system. In the early 1990s there was an upsurge of racially motivated violence against Maghrebian young people in Anderlecht, usually initiated by white young people and adults, and reports of police racism. This culminated in 1996 in an incident in which a 16-year- old Moroccan boy was shot dead by police. This incident triggered a renewed spate of violent inter-racial conflict. The local authority, fearing that this would further isolate the Moroccan inhabitants of the commune, compounding their 'ghettoisation', initiated a nine-pronged programme (see Figure 9.3).

Over the period the Anderlecht Initiative has made a significant impact upon violent youth crime, drop-out rates, educational attainment and employment, which we discuss later in this chapter.

Shared ownership and leadership

As we have noted, the OJJDP Comprehensive Gang Strategy in the USA identifies community mobilisation as a prerequisite of success and stresses that local citizens and organisations should *be* 'involved in a common enterprise ... working as a team'. This enables the

- The establishment of a *Mission Locale* with responsibility for economic and social regeneration.

- Environmental improvements to neighbourhood streets and open spaces.

- Housing refurbishment.

- Community diversification to attract residents from a broader range of socio-economic backgrounds.

- The democratisation of schools through the creation of schools councils for students and greater parental involvement and representation.

- A 'social contract' initiative involving street-based youth workers, which aimed to defuse potentially violent situations and divert young people to recreational cultural and sporting activities. Street *Educateurs* targeted hot spots of violence and accompanied mainly white football fans to and from matches at the Anderlecht football stadium in order to avert violence.

- A vocational training initiative that aimed to popularise vocational training by linking closely with local employers. This initiative targeted Moroccan young people and aimed to reduce their high school and college drop-out rate.

- A local 'active labour market' strategy to create primary sector work for young people completing vocational training.

- The introduction of 'mediators' in secondary and tertiary education, which aimed to prevent violence in schools.

Figure 9.3   The Anderlecht Initiative

initiative to remain anchored in day-to-day reality, thereby achieving the necessary credibility. If, however, the initiative is to retain the support and involvement of the young people and adults caught up in the gang problem, their involvement must go beyond mere tokenism, not least because the evidence suggests that genuine political participation can serve to reduce crime and violence in the poorest neighbourhoods (Crimmens 2004). Sherry Arnstein (1969) provided a salutary 'ladder of citizen participation' against which to measure the degree of participation to be ceded to the partners in and subjects of an intervention (Figure 9.4).

However, to share power with previously marginalised people, some of whom come from 'the other side of the fence', can be difficult for those in government and public service in our increasingly

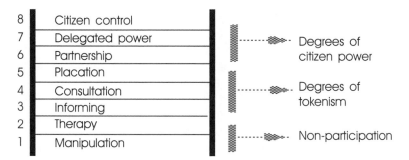

Figure 9.4 A ladder of citizen participation

'risk-averse' society (Beck 1992). Yet, as the experience of MMAGS suggests, effective work with gangs requires that we take risks. Face-to-face work with volatile, and sometimes armed, young people is risky. Giving public money to gang-involved young people to start a social enterprise is risky. Taking them on as interns or apprentices means that the council's insurance premium will rise. But without taking risks, effective work with armed, gang-involved young people will be difficult, if not impossible.

If the partnership is to flourish, it will be important that the initiative is not seen to be located, administratively, within the criminal justice system, since this may well deter participation by would-be community activists and young people who are, or have been, involved in gangs or with the criminal justice system.

Moreover, perceived criminal justice connections might well provoke a negative response from those young people targeted by the initiative. A gang desistance programme in White borough utilises the skills of criminal justice professionals but retains an identity separate from the criminal justice system and this enables it to make and sustain contact with young people heavily involved with gangs and gun crime. In an adjacent borough, an exemplary gun crime project that utilises the skills of a range of voluntary sector programmes struggles to attract these 'hard core' young people, despite participation being voluntary, because of the perception, born of its referral system, that it is more closely associated with the criminal justice system than it actually is.

Although partnership working is essential, it is not without its problems. Sometimes different agencies have differing levels of commitment to an initiative because the problem or issue the partnership is constructed to address may have a high priority for one but not for another. As a result, their investment in the partnership will be determined by whether and to what extent it enables them to fulfil their core objectives and meet their 'key performance indicators' (KPIs). Such differential commitment finds expression in poor attendance at meetings, sequential attendance wherein agencies send different representatives to each meeting, or attendance by low-status agency representatives who are not mandated to make decisions or commit resources. It may also be expressed as a reluctance or failure to contribute the promised resources. This serves to undermine trust between the partners and may in extreme cases jeopardise the initiative.

Some respondents suggested that voluntary sector organisations and community groups entering multi-agency partnerships often failed to appreciate the extent to which targets and KPIs have become a driving force in statutory agencies. They noted that sometimes voluntary organisations or community groups are effectively 'hijacked' by the statutory partner, who surreptitiously steers the project or initiative towards the achievement of their centrally prescribed targets, irrespective of its local relevance.

Several respondents, including some young people, commented that statutory criminal justice agencies and local authorities are sometimes happy enough to utilise the skills, knowledge and local credibility of voluntary sector and community groups and the young people themselves in order to realise their policy objectives, or to give the impression that they are active in areas where they are not, but far less willing to involve them in framing policy.

Respondents in all three boroughs expressed concern that the needs of young people were sometimes subordinated to the bureaucratic imperatives of statutory agencies bent on 'ticking boxes'. The constraints imposed by the justice system were a particular cause for concern and one respondent commented:

In the justice system, there is a need for a changed focus on long-term outcomes rather than the achievement of short-term targets.

They said that work with multiply disadvantaged young people often requires workers to 'go the extra mile' but that institutional culture and the constraints of court orders and the like can make this difficult. This can demoralise the workers and this in turn feeds the sense of fatalism that many of the young people feel. This suggests that partnership-building may require more time and attention than it often receives.

Family support

Many parents whose children are gang involved or gang affected feel unable to exert the control and influence they would wish and this can engender a sense of inadequacy that may undermine their coping capacities. This can lead to family conflict and in some cases young people may vacate or be 'thrown out' of their homes. These parents need support, yet support from statutory agencies is usually only forthcoming if they become the subjects of a potentially stigmatising 'parenting order' imposed by a court (Goldson 2002).

These families may also need help with the nuts and bolts of daily life, to find out about the state benefits and state services to which they are entitled. They may need advocacy in the areas of benefits, housing, education and childcare. Beyond this they may also need assistance with financial management and information about the educational, recreational and vocational opportunities available to them and their children.

From Autumn 2007 the National Parenting Academy has offered social care professionals specific advice and training on work with families of African and Caribbean origin. However, the House of Commons Select Committee Report, *Black Young People and the Criminal Justice System* (2007), recommends that in order to overcome potential recipients' suspicions of statutory agencies, they should make greater use of third-sector organisations that offer parenting programmes, and in particular black voluntary, community and faith groups. However, for this to become a reality it will be necessary to build the capacity of these groups and organisations.

As noted earlier, parents under these sorts of pressures often experience a sense of isolation, even though other parents in their neighbourhoods are subject to the same pressures. This is one of the reasons why neighbourhood capacity-building initiatives have sometimes grown out of family support programmes.

Neighbourhood capacity building

As we have seen, on some housing estates in Red, White and Blue boroughs there are acute pressures on children and young people to become involved with violent youth gangs. Thus a key to stemming the flow is helping residents combat these pressures. Neighbourhood capacity building utilises existing social networks to connect with neighbourhood residents with in-depth knowledge of their area, its inhabitants and the problems they confront. It endeavours to enable people to exert greater influence upon the policies affecting their neighbourhoods, the strategies devised by criminal justice, social welfare and educational and employment agencies and organisations, and the manner of their implementation. It does this by equipping residents with the knowledge and skills that will enable them to make an impact in the places where key decisions affecting them, their children and their neighbourhoods are made.

Following a serious assault on an estate in Red borough, parents, with the support of the housing association, the police and a local youth work training college, started a project called 'Reclaiming our Estate'. Adult residents and children and young people from the estate, some of whom were gang-involved, entered a dialogue with local authority service chiefs, ward councillors and the police about the impact of gang violence on residents' quality of life. This initiative culminated in extensive improvements to the fabric of the estate and its facilities, changes in policing styles, information-sharing protocols, improved youth and pre-school facilities and the closer involvement of ward councillors.

In some areas, police Safer Neighbourhood Teams have taken the lead in encouraging local people to express their concerns. However, for local people to give unequivocal messages to gang-involved young people, and information about gang activity to the police and other agencies, both key elements in Operation Ceasefire, they must have confidence that those agencies are prepared to remain involved until the threat has abated, and that police powers will be used fairly. Moreover, given the legacy of poor relations between the police and the black community, it is crucial that police action is not, and is not perceived to be, racially discriminatory. Indeed, in Boston the police expended a great deal of effort in the early stages of the programme trying to regain the trust of black residents in gang-affected neighbourhoods.

Many residents also feel that their voices are unheard in the places where key decisions about their plight are made. This would suggest that the high-profile involvement of local politicians acting as advocates for people in gang-affected neighbourhoods would be central to the success of any such initiative.

As we have noted, the predicament of residents is compounded by stigma and isolation and an important part of capacity building in these neighbourhoods will therefore concern reconnecting residents with educational, training, recreational and vocational opportunities beyond the neighbourhood.

Educational interventions

Many schools in Red, White and Blue boroughs are not only struggling with the adverse effects of gang culture upon their students, but also with the problems of under-achievement, truancy, school exclusion, and student–student and staff–student conflict.

In Belgium in the late 1990s the central government invested substantial sums of money to reduce educational drop-out and truancy among ethnic and cultural minorities and other socially disadvantaged students. In Anderlecht teachers and other professionals recognised that to achieve this objective it would be necessary to create a mechanism whereby the school, its students, their parents and the other social welfare and criminal justice agencies with which young people had dealings could be drawn into a dialogue. It was this recognition that spawned the role of the educational mediator in the Anderlecht educational system.

This element of the Anderlecht Initiative has a particular relevance for schools in the Red, White and Blue boroughs because it addresses problems raised repeatedly by professionals and parents there: namely, how to make and sustain contact with those children and young people who are excluded from school or exclude themselves, or are to all intents and purposes lost to the education system altogether as a result of familial disaffection and transience. The Anderlecht Initiative demonstrates that it is possible to re-establish contact with these disenchanted, gang-involved, young people and reintroduce them to relevant education, training and employment (Pitts and Porteous 2005).

A crucial ingredient of the Anderlecht Initiative was the placement of mediators in schools and vocational colleges. The mediation scheme proceeded from the assumption that second- and third-generation Maghrebian children and young people were not only excluded from the sociocultural, educational and economic mainstream; in many cases they were also estranged from their parents and their culture of origin. Thus there was a need for people who understood these difficulties 'from the inside' to help bridge the gap.

At the start of the initiative, 28 mediators were employed in schools, 14 Belgian and 14 Moroccan. The 14 Moroccan mediators were all men and they were sent into schools with a high proportion of Moroccan students and problems of violence.

Their primary role was to facilitate communication between the students and the school, the school and the family and, sometimes, between the family and the child or young person. As they became established their role broadened to include mediation between the young people, their families and the external environment: the police, health, welfare and housing services and potential employers. As time has gone by, the list of their duties has grown to include establishing partnerships and projects in the neighbourhood. The responsibilities cited most often by mediators are:

• Mediating between young people involved in violence.
• Mediating between young people and the school in cases of truancy.
• Facilitating communication between teachers and students.
• Facilitating communication between schools and families.
• Facilitating communication between psychological, medical and social services, children, young people and families.
• Facilitating communication between young people and employers.
• Keeping contact with children and young people in conflict with the school.
• Keeping contact with children and young people likely to drop out of school.
• Keeping contact with children and young people who have dropped out of school or college.

It is their positioning between the school on the one hand and the children and young people on the other that differentiates this new kind of professional from, for example, the mentor, the educational social worker, or the connexions adviser. Mediators have a loose accountability to headteachers but are employed by the municipality in order to vouchsafe their independence. As we have seen, the mediation scheme in Anderlecht was part of a broader, layered initiative. In their assessment of its impact, Pitts and Porteous (2005) point to the following factors that accounted for its success:

• It is holistic. It addresses social, cultural and economic factors simultaneously.
• It involves students as partners in developing the initiative.
• It engages professionals in a process of change, adaptation and dialogue with students.
• It reconfigures professional boundaries to ensure that appropriate mixes of skills, knowledge and authority are brought to bear on problems.

- It uses mediators to develop partnerships between the key stakeholders and to articulate a range of individuals, services and resources into the 'minimum sufficient network' (Skynner 1971) necessary to address the complex problems confronted by the children and young people.

In London, the over-representation of African-Caribbean young people in violent youth gangs tends to mask the reality that a substantial minority of them are first-generation migrants, in many instances coming from the war zones of Africa. These groups, particularly if they entered the country illegally or as unaccompanied minors, tend to be transient and as such elusive. It is unlikely that many of these young people could be reached via mainstream services and so, if this is to happen at all, we may need to recruit the kinds of street-based mediators or *Educateurs*/youth workers deployed in Anderlecht, who are drawn from these communities and understand the ethnic and cultural backgrounds, the experiences and the lives lived by these young people.

Downsizing the educational experience

Many parents, teachers and school governors interviewed in Red, White and Blue boroughs believed that gang-involved young people who drop out of secondary education might have been held there by a more 'child-centred' educational experience, conducted in smaller groups by one or two teachers, pursuing a more relevant and accessible curriculum: one that started 'where they are', both socially and academically.

Den Helder is a coastal town in the north-east of Holland where around 5 per cent of the population is of Dutch-Caribbean and Maghrebian origin. There is a thriving hard drugs market in the town and drug-related gun crime has been a problem there. Since the mid 1990s, Den Helder has seen a steady trickle of refugees and asylum-seekers from conflict zones in the Balkans, Africa and the Middle East. These groups tend to be poorer than their White Dutch neighbours, more likely to experience problems in education and employment and to fall foul of the law.

The large secondary school that serves the town caters for approximately 1,000 students between the ages of 12 and 15. However, it operates a range of special programmes for 'socially excluded' and socially disadvantaged children and young people, including recently arrived refugees and asylum-seekers. While none of these programmes targets a particular racial group, young people of Dutch-Caribbean and Maghrebian origin are heavily represented in them.

Students experiencing difficulty coping with the behavioural and/or academic demands of mainstream school life are offered the opportunity to pursue a simplified, integrated educational curriculum (known as BD). The students opting for BD tend to be those most 'at risk' in a variety of ways and, as the director of the unit says, 'most in need of care'. BD students have a limited school day: 9.00–2.30 rather than 9.00–4.00, because they tend to lose concentration. Some students pursue an even more restricted programme of only 12 hours per week if they are unable to cope with full-time schooling. Each BD student has a dedicated teacher who meets them at the end of each school day for 'debriefing'.

The BD programmes are taught in a dedicated wing of the school, and in common with other school departments BD has its own director. The emphasis in class is upon the development of transferable skills and the attitudes that will enable students to succeed in school and beyond. The first skill to be taught is independent learning. Groups of students undertake research in their neighbourhoods, which requires them to use maths, history, Dutch, etc. Local shopkeepers and industrialists are often involved in these projects and towards the end of the course may be asked to stage job interviews to allow students to gain an appreciation of the demands that will be made upon them out in the world of work.

BD classes are taught by a small group of half a dozen teachers on a thematic, rather than subject-specific, basis over two years. The BD staff group is trying to promote a cultural shift using teacher self-evaluation instruments and peer review. Teachers attend one another's lessons and this appears to be transforming the ethos of teaching in the whole school. One result of this is that teachers teaching high-achieving students are also tending to utilise thematic approaches to the curriculum and a more child-centred pedagogy, emphasising participative learning and the development of a broader range of social and academic skills by students. The BD director said:

This is participatory education that uses students' own experience or simulations which give the students these experiences. Teachers are getting better at picking up issues raised by students.

The school retains the services of Kardeel Youth Care, an NGO that has transformed itself from an off-site day-care service for excluded school students into an agency that also places 'youth care' professionals in schools. As the manager of Kardeel observed:

Now, problematic youngsters are worked with to keep them in school rather than when they fall out of school. I work with students, individually and in groups, from all levels of the school, not just BD students, but mainly with those BD students at greatest risk of dropping out.

Although students may be referred to Kardeel by teachers, their involvement is always voluntary. The worker, who is a trained child psychologist, undertakes an assessment of the situation or issue with the children and may then devise a strategy involving the child, the teacher, and the family as well if the student agrees. These plans, or contracts, usually concern the attendance and behaviour of the child but they can also cover commitments made by parents and teachers and the nature of the work the Kardeel worker will do with them.

Most of the students Kardeel works with have a negative view of school and often only attend because their friends do. The main issues worked with are behaviour, relationships with teachers, relationships with families, bullying and choice-making. The sessions may focus on social and emotional skills, help with homework, the student's situation at home or at school, sometimes using role-play. The worker aims to identify areas of achievement with the student in order to maximise their satisfaction with school.

Kardeel offers an independent mediation and advocacy service, recognising that some students, particularly those in the BD programme, will sometimes come into conflict with the school, and their own families, and that at these times they will need independent support and advocacy. As with the mediators in Anderlecht, the independence of the Kardeel counsellor is important because this allows him or her to be critical of the school. Counsellors will sometimes tell the school if they think it is generating problems for students. However, as one counsellor observed:

For this to happen there must be open discussion and I must earn the respect of the teachers.

Although these conflicts can generate some friction between the Kardeel counsellor and school staff, the school authorities recognise that this is inevitable, and necessary, if the most disaffected young people are to be kept in the school.

If a child cannot be worked with in the school, consultants, employed by the local authority to fulfil its legal responsibility to provide full-time education for all school-age children, endeavour to find or create an alternative route to a vocational qualification. This may involve referral to a special educational and training project, also run by Kardeel, thus ensuring some continuity. The consultants are required by law to ensure that no child is excluded from a school without an alternative route to a vocational qualification having been arranged.

The key features of the Den Helder intervention are:

- The school provides a variety of educational regimes designed to suit young people of differing needs and abilities.

- Specialist workers in liaison with voluntary sector projects devise alternative routes for the young people who cannot be dealt with effectively in schools.

- Dialogue between teachers concerning the development and refinement of techniques and interventions is supported by the school.

The Black voluntary sector and the school

The House of Commons Home Affairs Select Committee 2007 Report *Young Black People and the Criminal Justice System* points to the need for improved links between the black voluntary sector and schools and in particular the ways in which the sector might be involved in developing alternatives to school exclusion. To this end it recommends that government should research the impact of supplementary schools, provided within the black community, and promote co-operation and collaboration between supplementary schools and mainstream education. It also commends the introduction of independent lay mentors into schools with a high proportion of BME students.

Likewise, the REACH Report, published in August 2007 by The Men's Room, a consortium of successful black businessmen and professionals, recommends reducing the barriers faced by black parents and families by building stronger parent–teacher relationships. This should be achieved via 'a national framework of family–school partnerships, ensuring that the specific needs of Black families are integral to the framework'. The REACH Report also argues for increasing parental engagement, the creation of parent-centred learning workshops and the encouragement of more black parents to become school governors, teaching assistants and teachers.

Dealing with the feelings

However, black parent governors in Blue borough suggested that, because many African-Caribbean people have experienced racism in the British educational system they are sceptical about whether they can achieve success via the normal institutional routes. This belief, they said, is communicated in subtle and sometimes not so subtle, ways to the younger generation and it is compounded by the messages these young people are picking up in the secondary school playground from year 7 onwards. One consequence of this scepticism is to limit the flow of young black men entering the teaching profession. Yet what is needed, they believe, is a 'critical mass' of reliable and concerned black male teachers who will work with the most disaffected black boys throughout their life at secondary school.

These respondents argue that if black men are to be reconnected with the educational mainstream, a place that many have experienced as a site of failure and humiliation, it may be necessary to create safe spaces where they can discuss these issues and get a collective sense of the damage that their experiences in the education system have done. Respondents felt very strongly that an inter-generational dialogue needed to be opened up in which black children and young people could gain an awareness of the struggles of their forebears, a sense that they are implicated in the same struggle, and that the older generation should express solidarity, and work with them to devise solutions that are not self-defeating. But how are these disaffected black men to be reconnected with educational institutions?

ARCES is a charitable organisation based in Palermo, Sicily, which aims to prevent school failure and marginalisation by involving families (usually parents but also other relatives if necessary) in these processes. The project has three main objectives:

- To encourage the participation of parents and teachers of pupils at risk in activities focused on parenting, education and health, in an attempt to improve the school's relationship with families.

- To enhance the families' understanding of and commitment to their children's education.

147

- To learn from families' experiences to develop empowering solutions to the difficulties they face.

The target group for this project is the families of children of compulsory school age (6–15 years) identified as being 'at risk' of dropping out of school or who had already done so. The project worked in the poorest regions of Palermo, characterised by high levels of absolute and relative poverty and disadvantage. The families were drawn largely from a group of poor rural people who were stigmatised because of their poverty and their distinctive dialect. These people had often had negative experiences of education and tended not to value it as a resource.

The project intervenes at a number of different levels with individual children and young people, with their families, school staff and in the administration of the school. Project staff argue that intervening on only one of these levels would be insufficient, because the project's philosophy is that the individual child or young person's problems must be understood and responded to within this wider social context.

Intervention with families takes two forms: counselling with individuals and families and group work, in which parents from several families discuss issues. These sessions are sometimes very emotional, as parents share information about their own schooldays, which were often experiences of humiliation and failure. They bring feelings of anger, resentment and frustration as well as their sense of failure. For many this is the first time they have expressed these feelings and they are almost always surprised to discover that other group members share them. From this, it is often possible to move on to a discussion of how parental experiences have influenced the messages they are giving to their children. The next step is to bring the parents into the school in a teaching role, to share their experiences and impart their skills. Group discussions among families are routinely used to evaluate the programme and whole-group discussions with teachers are used in the same way. These discussions reveal qualitative changes in attitudes towards schools and their staff and staff attitudes to parents and children. Recent participants (parents) have said the programme:

- *Allowed me to express my terrible experiences at school for the first time ever.*
- *Made me feel so much better, healthier, I feel transformed.*

- *Made me feel 'important'.*
- *Helped me overcome my nervousness and feel more confident.*
- *Helped me make new friends.*
- *Helped me to feel an equal member of the group.*

Teachers reported an enhanced ability to relate to socially disadvantaged students and their families, greater confidence in teaching them and heightened expectations. For its part, the ARCES programme has now been mainstreamed into Palermo secondary schools.

The key features of the ARCES programme are:

- The educational experiences of parents are used as a starting point for understanding children's attitudes to and problems with education.

- Parents are offered opportunities to discover that other parents of similar social and cultural origin, and in a similar situation, had similarly damaging educational experiences and that this is not simply their problem.

- Parents are consulted about how they would like the educational system to operate for their children.

- Parents are involved as partners and active participants in the development of their child's school career.

- Educational psychologists act as mediators between home and school and also support teachers in their dealings with hard-to-handle youngsters in the classroom.

- Systematic evaluation indicates that the methods employed are effective in mobilising parents as an educational resource and as a support for children and young people who themselves feel alienated from school.

School-based gang strategies

Some schools and FE colleges have a 'gang problem', in the sense that gang activity and gang conflict occurs within the school. Others, while not having a problem in school, have to deal with the impact of gangs on their students and their students' parents. Others appear to be largely unaffected, but whether a school or college is affected by gangs or not is primarily a matter of geography. However, pressures to maximise year 7 intake and minimise school exclusions may cause gang-affected schools to deny or minimise the impact of gangs. In the USA, Stover (1986) found that districts unused to gang activity may be reluctant to acknowledge its appearance. He cites Roberto Rivera, director of the Chicago Intervention Network, who urged school boards to encourage administrators to be alert for signs of gang activity and assure them that reporting problems won't reflect adversely on them. Gang-affected schools, and their staff, need the support of the education authority, other schools and other agencies if they are to combat the problem, and this is beginning to happen in the Red, White and Blue boroughs.

US research suggests that gang-affected schools and colleges can adopt effective strategies to minimise the impact of gangs (Lal and Lal 1995; Lal 1996) if, at the outset, they adopt an attitude that mirrors that of the gang. That is:

> There is nothing more important than our gang.
>
> vs
>
> There is nothing more important than our school.

The research suggests that an Operational Team, comprising the head or principal, the school administrator, a school police officer or one linked to the school for the purpose, staff with responsibilities for pastoral care, counselling, home–school liaison, etc., parents and representatives from a youth justice agency, be brought into being to create what we might call the 'minimum sufficient network' necessary to address the problem (Skynner 1971). This Operational Team would be formally linked into the broader multi-agency gang strategy. The Operational Team's job would be to:

- Establish information flow between all parties. Stover (1986) cites the Milwaukee school security chief Jerry Mourning, who urges schools to keep abreast of gang rivalries:

  You need to know what's happening in the community. What happens over the weekend, we handle on Monday mornings.

  In Chicago, the school board receives monthly reports on student assaults from each school to give them an overview of city-wide trends (Stover 1986).

- Analyse the school environment with respect to the extent and intensity of gang activity.

- Formulate goals and objectives that are realistic and measurable.

- Devise a strategy.

- Monitor and measure its impact.

- Revise and refine the strategy in the light of measured impact and the changing nature of the problem.

Most US research suggests that schools must be established as neutral ground, a strategy adopted in several secondary schools in Red, White and Blue boroughs. Anything related to gang membership should be banned: weapons, violence, illegal activity, gang-identified clothing, insignia and gestures. Graffiti should be painted over immediately. Not only does this signal that school property is not the gang's, it also discourages rival gangs from responding with more graffiti, or worse, defacing their rival's symbols, which can lead to retaliation and violence.

Anti-gang policies in Portland, Oregon, for example, included searching students and their lockers if there were indications of drugs or weapons, and expelling and referring to juvenile justice agencies any student found to possess weapons (McKinney 1988). However, because many young people in gang-affected neighbourhoods in London carry weapons for self-defence or under pressure from gang-involved peers, such a strategy if ruthlessly pursued could generate a sense of injustice that would limit information flow, thereby rendering them even less safe.

Staff can expect to be tested constantly by the subtle and changing forms of gang symbols. It is obviously important, therefore, that schools communicate clear, consistent standards of discipline and enforce them. A study of Ohio gang activity found that teachers who backed down in confrontations were more likely to be assaulted than teachers who were firm but fair (Bryant 1989).

Some US school districts split up gangs by transferring disruptive students, but although this may reduce friction Spergel (1989) warns that new problems sometimes result, particularly if a gang member is transferred to a school dominated by another gang.

Preventive and diversionary initiatives are also important. Chicago schools offer recreational alternatives to gang activity by staying open for evening extra-curricular activities, as the 'extended school' is intended to do in the UK.

Reconnecting with opportunity

In Chapter 8 we described some of the deleterious effects of living in gang-affected neighbourhoods. Evidence of the 'neighbourhood effect' is provided by the US federal government's Moving to Opportunity (MTO) experimental mobility programme, which investigated the fortunes of people who moved from poor and dangerous neighbourhoods to more prosperous and safer ones. The researchers found that moving to socially mixed, 'non-poor' areas produced significant positive effects on child and adult physical and mental health, children's behaviour, their involvement in crime and exposure to violent victimisation (Del Conte and Kling 2001). These families were also more likely to become economically self-sufficient and to earn higher salaries (Galster and Zobel 1998; Leventhal and Brooks-Gunn 2001). Much of this improvement is attributable to the fact that the neighbourhoods to which the ghetto-dwellers moved were connected into local economies.

However, with escalating property prices and 1,500,000 people on UK council housing waiting lists, 'moving to opportunity' will be an option only for the lucky few. In which case, given the link between concentrated youth unemployment and gang involvement, reconnecting gang-affected neighbourhoods with local labour markets would appear to be a priority.

The high level of black and mixed heritage youth unemployment in the Red, White and Blue boroughs, its contribution to young people's decision to affiliate to gangs and their failure to desist from membership points to the centrality of coherent and creative employment strategies to effective gang interventions.

There are some positive signs. Current government employment policy is founded in the notion that work is the best way out of poverty, and so labour market intervention is increasingly targeted at the most disadvantaged. Neighbourhood renewal is being refocused with a greater emphasis on tackling worklessness. Moreover, social housing policy is acknowledging that for neighbourhoods to stabilise, social landlords will need to tackle high levels of worklessness and benefit dependency among their tenants (Pitts 2008).

Recent community consultation exercises have found widespread support for measures of this type. However, there is a need to tackle the mismatch between the skills offered by this potential workforce and those demanded by potential employers. Several respondents bemoaned the short-term nature of much statutory work with gang-involved young people because it did not allow sufficient time for the acquisition of the requisite skills for survival in the workplace. A respondent in White borough said:

Some of these young people have absolutely nothing in place: no national insurance number, no bank account, or driving licence. We have to teach them basic skills that they should have had before they arrived at the programme and this is very frustrating.

Another observed that his agency's most needy young people

... are months, maybe years, away from 'square one' and we need programmes that will stick with them until they can get there.

Others argued that once in the workplace these young people required continuing support from project workers in what is likely to be a difficult transition.

While the obvious response would be to 'upskill' these young people, those most in need of training are often the most disaffected and as such, unlikely to take advantage of programmes that they believe, on past experience, will yield little more than a certificate of attendance.

In the near future, the government plans to raise the age of compulsory education and training to 18. While this could, theoretically, hold an answer to the 'skills deficit' problem, unless the programmes on offer are very different from these young people's experience of school or vocational training programmes, it could also generate all kinds of problems for the young people and those endeavouring to train them.

In Belgium, student selection occurs at the age of 15, and students between 15 and 18 years old who are not proceeding to higher education are required to attend vocational college on one or two days a week and to undertake a work placement on two or three days a week. The majority of ethnic and cultural minority young people follow this vocational route. However, in recent years, the annual drop-out rate from vocational colleges has been very high, between 30 per cent and 50 per cent. These high drop-out rates are attributable to the traditional unpopularity of the colleges with students, who have seen attendance as a mark of failure. As a result, many left without a vocational certificate, which means that in a situation where primary sector employment opportunities are scarce they are unlikely to secure the kind of job they want, or indeed any job at all.

The head of one Anderlecht vocational college said that over 90 per cent of his students were drawn from ethnic minorities, mainly from the Maghreb. He noted that in the mid 1990s there had been problems of violence, class control and truancy at the college because:

> *Technical education was viewed as a negative choice, something to do if you had failed in mainstream education. The training itself was second-rate and the professions to which it gave entry were regarded by students as third-rate.*

In the mid 1990s teachers in these colleges went on strike in protest at the violence directed towards them and their students.

As a result, the national government attempted to change the image of technical education through a publicity campaign, featuring successful graduates who were working in skilled and well-paid jobs, and economic interventions that aimed to generate more better-paid skilled jobs in areas of high immigrant settlement. For its part, the vocational colleges introduced greater student choice, and participation in decision-making, and refined down the training options to those that led to reasonably paid local employment. A college principal said:

> *This led to a situation in which larger numbers of students were opting into technical and vocational education rather than being 'bounced out' of the educational mainstream into it. New systems of peer review of teaching were introduced so that teachers could learn from one another how to engage 'challenging' students. Teachers experiencing problems were given special coaching. Mediators were appointed to liaise with families, work-experience placements and employers who could offer jobs to graduates.*
>
> *The idea was to create a partnership between students, their families and local employers. The partnership between employers and the Moroccan community in general has become very strong.*

Thus the mediator attempted to build the 'minimum sufficient networks' (Skynner 1971) necessary to bind the young person into education and training, using the services of psychologists or social workers as necessary, if agreed with the young person. The college principal noted:

It is important that nobody should feel alone and everybody has full information. This is particularly important when crises arise. Getting the employers to feel part of the partnership is crucial and this is a central role of the mediator.

This suggests a need for targeted interventions that offer alternative routes into attainment and work at an earlier stage. These interventions need to be attractive, offering realistic opportunities for reasonably paid, permanent employment in the local economy.

In most inner London boroughs the local authority is the largest employer, yet few have schemes that recruit gang-involved young people into public sector employment. As of February 2008, however, White borough has included the development of local government apprenticeships and internships in its gang strategy. Most local authorities also operate Employer of Choice initiatives which, if linked into gang strategies, could offer highly desirable 'PR' and 'branding' opportunities to those businesses.

However, in some cases effective employment initiatives need to play to the cultural strengths and lifestyles of the young people they are aimed at. In Milwaukee, for example, John Hagedorn (1998) developed a website-building factory for gang-involved young people who agreed to desist from gang violence. This project played to their interest in the technology, their individualistic orientation and their idiosyncratic timeframes. The factory was open 24 hours a day and they could come and go as they pleased, but were only paid on the basis of what they produced.

Many respondents suggested that social enterprises of this type, where gang-involved young people could become partners, with a stake in the business and be able to earn a decent wage legitimately, were urgently needed. Happily, there are several not-for-profit organisations, like 'Bright Ideas', run by the first winner of the hit TV show *The Apprentice*, Tim Campbell, that will both advance capital and provide mentors, successful business people, to support young, socially disadvantaged, entrepreneurs.

Youth and community work

The OJJDP programmes in the USA, described above, targeted young people who were unable to connect with mainstream institutions, offering them individualised, age-appropriate, social, educational and vocational opportunities on the basis of an assessment of their needs and abilities.

In Red, White and Blue boroughs, some gang programmes target young people heavily involved with gangs and gun crime, while others respond to the fears, needs and ambitions of children and young people growing up in gang-affected neighbourhoods. However, it is evident that despite the important work they are doing these programmes do not, in the present circumstances, represent a comprehensive gang initiative. This is because of:

- The paucity and uncertainty of the financial support available to them.
- A lack of co-ordination of their efforts.
- The absence of information-sharing protocols with the police and other criminal justice agencies.
- A lack of relevant up-to-date intelligence about gang activity that would enable them to mount sustained, targeted interventions in particular neighbourhoods/locations.
- The absence of a shared risk/need assessment framework with which to devise interventions for targeted groups and individuals.
- The absence of a systematic programme of monitoring and evaluation to serve as a basis for decisions about service provision.

This suggests a need for comprehensive, 'layered' youth work provision that is both preventive and responsive, targeting those involved in gang and gun crime and those affected by it (see Figure 9.5).

Level 1 interventions would target gang Elders and the most heavily involved Youngers known to the police; Priority and Prolific Offender Projects (PPOs); Intensive Supervision and Surveillance Programmes (ISSPs); street-based youth workers; and voluntary sector projects. They would target not only adjudicated offenders but those who, although heavily involved in gang crime, have evaded apprehension. The intervention would focus upon enforcement, intensive problem-solving, mediation and the development of alternative futures, via education, training and employment.

It is at levels 1 and 2 that discussion between the police, the youth service and social welfare agencies concerning the relative merits of enforcement action or social intervention in any given case, would take place.

At level 2 a useful vehicle for interventions with Youngers and certain Wannabes at serious risk of heavy involvement in gangs would

	The intervention	The target group
Level 1	PPO/police/ISSPs and specialist voluntary/ third sector organisations	Targeted intensive interventions with core gang members (Elders/ Youngers)/prolific violent offenders. Enforcement and/or intensive social intervention involving problem-solving, mediation and the development of alternative futures via education, training and employment.
Level 2	YIP/extended school/FE colleges/university Aim Higher programmes and specialist voluntary/ third-sector organisations	Targeted interventions with Youngers and Wannabes seriously 'at risk' of involvement. Intensive problem-solving and the development of alternative futures via education, training and employment.
Level 3	Youth Service Outreach Team/YISP	Targeted interventions with moderately 'at risk', gang-involved groups, Tinys and younger siblings. Problem-oriented and social-educational interventions
Level 4	Housing associations/ schools Youth Service/ Sports clubs/voluntary/ third-sector organisations	Area/school-based social-educational/recreational youth and community interventions directed towards gang-affected young people.

Figure 9.5 A four-level gang intervention model

be the type of Youth Inclusion Programmes (YIPs) introduced into 70 high-crime neighbourhoods in 1999 by the Youth Justice Board. YIPs target a core group of 50 young people, deemed by a multi-agency panel to be those most 'at risk'. In addition to the core 50, a broader group of up to 150 young people, usually friends or associates of the core group, is encouraged to participate in YIP activities. As with level 1 interventions, interventions at level 2 would focus upon intensive problem-solving, mediation and the development of alternative futures via education, training and employment. However, YIPs utilise a broad range of other methods and activities, including street-based youth work, counselling, mentoring, group work, outdoor activities, football tournaments and fashion shows, and in doing so manage to make and sustain contact with what is often a multiply disadvantaged and 'hard-to-reach' population. As well as enhancing their social lives, YIPs aim to reintroduce these young people to education, training or work (Morgan *et al.* 2003). However, as we suggested earlier, effective employment opportunities have to play to the cultural strengths of the young people they are aimed at and may involve basic skills education on the one hand and training people to become self-employed entrepreneurs on the other.

At level 3, interventions would target those on the periphery of gang involvement, who would be unlikely to find their own way into education, training or employment. This level of intervention would aim for reintegration into or support for participation in mainstream educational, recreational and vocational activity, probably utilising the mediators described above. Here too, targeted work with girls and young women involved in gangs, but not infrequently violently and sexually abused by gang members would be provided. Beyond this core group, however, are other girls and young women who live in gangland and are, as a result, exposed to heightened levels of intimidation, threat and abuse who also need support and protection.

Level 4 interventions would consist of 'universal' social-educational and recreational youth and community provision, but with a particular focus upon non-gang-involved children and young people, under pressure in gang-affected neighbourhoods.

Rehabilitation and resettlement

Adequate throughcare and aftercare arrangements for gang-involved young people when they return from penal institutions would be a key feature of any effective gang initiatives. Successful rehabilitation depends upon the quality of the work undertaken during the prison sentence and in the period following release, as well as close liaison between the prison and the youth offending or probation services.

Research indicates that desistance from future offending is most likely to occur if on release a young person's family situation is stable; they have somewhere decent to live; they have fulfilling work yielding an adequate income; any substance abuse problems are addressed; and they have access to social networks that offer non-criminal social and recreational opportunities (Farrall 2002). There are particular pressures on returning gang members, from their own and other gangs, and there is, of course, the ever-present temptation of easy money from the drugs business. It is for this reason that these young people may need a great deal of support during re-entry and this support may involve finding them accommodation outside their neighbourhood to avoid these pressures (Bateman and Pitts 2005). Effective intervention with returning gang members therefore requires co-ordination of a number of different agencies and the nomination of a key worker who will work with them intensively. This level of intervention may be beyond the capacities of the youth offending or probation services and it may therefore fall to workers from gang-desistance programmes to provide it. The intensity of such work would therefore need to be recognised in project funding and the training and support offered to project workers.

Intelligence, assessment and targeting

The development of a comprehensive strategy will require accurate up-to-date information about the activities of individuals and groups within gang-affected neighbourhoods. It would therefore be necessary to collect and collate data on gang-involved young people and young people at risk from gangs. Initially, it would be necessary to undertake research to establish the names, membership and location of gangs and offending youth groups, in order to assess threats, risks and needs, as a prelude to identifying targets for intervention, which would in turn determine the types of programmes to be commissioned. Alongside this, there would be a need to create, adopt or adapt a shared risk/needs assessment framework with which to devise interventions for targeted groups and individuals.

Monitoring and evaluation

In order to steer and develop an initiative with gang-involved and gang-affected young people, independent monitoring and evaluation of interventions and their impact is crucial. However, it is now fairly widely accepted that modes of research and evaluation utilised extensively in the justice system in recent years, which measure only inputs and outcomes but reveal little about how and why change occurs, are of little use to service-users, policy-makers, managers or practitioners (Pawson and Tilley 1997). Moreover, there is growing evidence that applied social research is most effective where service-users, managers and practitioners feel that they have some ownership of the research process. By involving these activists, it becomes possible to discover not just whether a particular intervention 'works' or not, but how and why it works, and how the lessons learned might be generalised to other settings. A further advantage of this approach is that it can give service-users an opportunity to formulate the questions to be asked and develop skills in research fieldwork and data analysis.

Commissioning and funding

There is a need to ensure the adequacy and duration of funding for effective and sustained intervention and the transparency and rationality of commissioning and funding decisions. For this to happen, funding and commissioning decisions would need to be made in the light of the intelligence data on service need and evaluation data on project or programme effectiveness.

Project infrastructure

Although most respondents were agreed that community and faith groups would be central to effective gang strategies, many of these groups lack the kinds of infrastructure that would enable effective project management. This can serve as a powerful disincentive to these groups embarking upon new ventures. In the recent past, funding regimes have worked against the development of 'grass-roots' community organisations and this has had a particularly deleterious effect on the Black voluntary sector. Short-term funding, a sometimes complex bidding process, lack of money to pay for independent monitoring and evaluation and the requirement to produce lengthy final reports, along with day-to-day administrative tasks concerning employment, salaries, national insurance, tax, etc., have effectively thwarted them.

In order to address this problem, there is the need for a central facility in gang-affected local authorities that would employ specialist workers to undertake programme support services (writing bids, commissioning, monitoring and evaluating the work, writing final reports, etc.) in partnership with small voluntary, community and faith groups. This facility would also employ and train young people and adults from gang-affected neighbourhoods, linking them into relevant courses in further and higher education. It would in addition provide 'back office' clerical services (salaries, national insurance, tax, accounts).

Youth and community work training

Many respondents suggested that effective gang-work requires a critical mass of young 'road people'. But for them to be effective it is necessary to create adequately resourced and academically accredited structures to handle their recruitment, training and professional supervision. In order to address this problem there is a need for another kind of central facility, available to all projects involved in the initiative, to play a training and staff supervision/staff development role with young 'road people' and other volunteers or trainees appointed by the commissioned agencies. This training function would be developed in partnership with training providers in further and higher education to ensure that volunteers and trainees receive forms of accreditation that enable them to progress to education and training in relevant fields.

Private troubles and public issues

This by no means exhaustive list of possible components of a gang strategy is offered tentatively. As we have argued, in violent youth gangs we confront a new kind of problem and none of us yet knows with any certainty what a solution would look like. Hence the need for experimentation and an openness to change.

Yet, one of the dangers of writing a 'What is to be done?' chapter like this is that the small army of shameless, entrepreneurial, academic and private sector claim-makers who stalk the youth justice system will, in accordance with the inexorable logic of the individualising imperative, abstract the cheapest, most readily do-able elements. They will transform them into 'assessment frameworks', 'programmes', 'packages', 'checklists', 'toolkits', and the usual array of anodyne performance indicators; which they will then endeavour to market to gullible criminal justice administrators under pressure to implement something that 'works'.

In so doing, public issues are translated back into private troubles and the rest of us are relieved of the responsibility of recognising that to some degree at least they, the young people trapped in gangland, are there because we are here; that the immiseration and danger they experience is inextricably linked to our prosperity and comparative safety.

We live in the middle of this carnage but for the most part we remain untouched by it. Usually we are no more than an audience in front of which these lethal dramas are enacted. Is this sense of separation because the young people involved are from a different social class; because they are a different colour; because they speak with a different lilt and find their cultural reference points in places unfamiliar to us? Whatever it is, this sense of separation is one of the reasons they are dying. Our moral choice is clear and can be stated succinctly: we must decide whether they are 'our' young people or not. And if we recognise that they are, we must turn the question of the social, economic and cultural conditions that propel them towards involvement in violent youth gangs into a burning public issue.

References

Adonis, A. and Pollard, S. (1998) *A Class Act: The Myth of Britain's Classless Society*. Harmondsworth: Penguin.

Anderson, S., Kinsey, R., Loader, I. and Smith, C. (1994) *Cautionary Tales: Young People, Crime and Policing in Edinburgh*. Aldershot: Avebury.

Arlacchi, P. (1998) 'Some Observations on Illegal Markets', in V. Ruggiero, N. South and I. Taylor (eds) *The New European Criminology*. London: Routledge.

Arnstein, S. (1969) 'A Ladder of Citizen Participation', *Journal of the American Planning Association*, 35 (4), July: 216–24.

Bateman, T. and Pitts, J. (2005) *The Russell House Companion to Youth Justice*. Lyme Regis: Russell House Publishing.

Baum, D. (1996) 'Can Integration Succeed? Research into Urban Childhood and Youth in a Deprived Area of Koblenz', *Social Work in Europe*, 3 (3).

Bauman, Z. (2004) *Wasted Lives*. Cambridge: Polity Press.

Beck, U. (1992) *The Risk Society: Towards a New Modernity*. London: Sage.

Becker, H. (1963) *Outsiders: Studies of the Sociology of Deviance*. New York: Free Press.

Belson, W. (1977) *Juvenile Theft: The Causal Factors*. London: Harper and Row.

Bloch, H. and Niederhoffer, A. (1958) *The Gang: A Study in Adolescent Behaviour*. New York: Philosophical Library.

Borges, J. L. *The Analytical Language of John Wilkins (El idioma analítico de John Wilkins)*. Oxford: Oxford University Press.

Bourdieu, P. (1998) *Acts of Resistance: Against the New Myths of Our Time*. Cambridge: Polity Press.

Bourgois, P. (1995) *In Search of Respect: Selling Crack in El Barrio*. Cambridge: Cambridge University Press.

Bowling, B. and Phillips, C. (2006) *Young Black People and the Criminal Justice System*, Submission to the Home Affairs Committee Inquiry (October).

Braga, A., Kennedy, D., Waring, E. and Piehl, A. (2001) 'Problem-oriented Policing, Deterrence, and Youth Violence: An Evaluation of Operation Ceasefire', *Journal of Research in Crime and Delinquency*, 38: 195–225.

Bryant, D. (1989) 'Community-wide Responses Crucial for Dealing with Youth Gangs', *Juvenile Justice Bulletin*, September: 1–6.

Bullock, K. and Tilley, N. (2003) *Shooting, Gangs and Violent Incidents in Manchester: Developing a Crime Reduction Strategy*. London: Home Office.

Burnett, R. and Appleton, C. (2004) *Joined-up Youth Justice: Tackling Youth Crime in Partnership*. Lyme Regis, Russell House Publishing.

Campbell, B. (1993) *Goliath: Britain's Dangerous Places*. London: Methuen.

Castells, M. (2000) *The Rise of the Network Society. The Information Age: Economy, Society and Culture*, Vol. 1. Oxford: Blackwell.

Cicourel, A. (1968) *The Social Organization of Juvenile Justice*. New York: John Wiley.

Clarke, C. (2006) 'Politics, Violence and Drugs in Kingston, Jamaica', *Bulletin of Latin American Research*, 25 (3), July: 420–40.

Clarke, J. (1975) 'Skinheads and the Magical Recovery of Community', in S. Hall and T. Jefferson (eds) *Resistance Through Rituals: Youth Subcultures in Post-war Britain*. London: Routledge.

Clarke, R. (1983) 'Situational Crime Prevention: Its Theoretical Basis and Practical Scope', in M. Tonry and N. Norris (eds) *Crime and Justice: An Annual Review of Research*, 4: 255–6.

Cloward, R. and Ohlin, L. (1960) *Delinquency and Opportunity*. London: Routledge and Kegan Paul.

Cohen, A. K. (1955) *Delinquent Boys: The Culture of the Gang*. New York: Free Press.

Cohen, A. and Taylor, E. (2000) *American Pharaoh: Mayor Richard J. Daley: His Battle for Chicago and the Nation*. New York: Little, Brown.

Coleman, J. S. (1999) 'Social Capital in the Creation of Human Capital', in P. Dasgupta and I. Serageldin (eds) *Social Capital: A Multifaceted Perspective*. World Bank Publications.

Cooper, A. and Lousada, J. (2005) *Borderline Welfare: Feeling and Fear of Feeling in Modern Welfare*. London: Karnac Books.

Corrigan, P. (1979) *Schooling the Smash Street Kids*. London: Macmillan.

Crimmens, D. (2004) *Having Their Say*. Lyme Regis: Russell House Publishing.

Crimmens, D., Factor, F., Jeffs, T., Pugh, C., Pitts, J., Spence, J. and Turner, P. (2004) *Reaching Socially Excluded Young People*. York: Joseph Rowntree Foundation/National Youth Bureau.

Currie, E. (1985) *Confronting Crime: An American Challenge*. New York: Pantheon.

Dahrendorf, R. (1994) 'The Changing Quality of Citizenship', in B. van Steenbergen (ed.) *The Condition of Citizenship*. London: Sage.

De Souza Briggs, X. (1998) 'Brown Faces in White Suburbs: Housing Mobility and the Many Faces of Social Capital', *Housing Policy Debate*, 9 (1): 177–221.

Dean, H. and Taylor-Gooby, P. (1992) *Dependency Culture: The Explosion of a Myth*. Hemel Hempstead: Harvester Wheatsheaf.

Dean, M. (1997) 'Tipping the Balance', *Search*, 27, Spring. Joseph Rowntree Foundation.

Decker, S., Bynum, T. and Weisel, D. (1998) 'A Tale of Two Cities as Organised Crime Groups', *Justice Quarterly*, 15: 395–425.

Decker, S. and Van Winkle, B. (1996) *Life in the Gang: Family, Friends and Violence*. Cambridge: Cambridge University Press.

Del Conte, A. and Kling, J. (2001) 'A Synthesis of MTO Research on Self Sufficiency, Safety and Health and Behaviour and Delinquency', *Poverty Research News*, 5 (1): 3–6.

Deschenes, E. and Esbensen, F. (1997) 'Saints, Delinquents, and Gang Members: Differences in Attitudes and Behavior', paper presented at the American Society of Criminology Annual Meeting, San Diego, CA.

Downes, D. (1966) *The Delinquent Solution*. London: Routledge and Kegan Paul.

Dukes, R., Martinez, R. and Stein, J. (1997) 'Precursors and Consequences of Membership in Youth Gangs', *Youth and Society*, 29 (2): 139–65.

Esbensen, F. (2000) 'Preventing Adolescent Gang Involvement', *OJJDP Juvenile Justice Bulletin*, US Department of Justice, Washington DC.

Farrall, S. (2002) *Rethinking What Works with Offenders: Probation, Social Context and Desistance from Crime*. Cullompton, Willan Publishing.

Farrington, D. (2002) 'Understanding and Preventing Youth Crime', in J. Muncie, G. Hughes and E. McLaughlin (eds) *Youth Justice: Critical Readings*. London: Sage.

Fawcett, B., Featherstone, B. and Goddard, J. (2004) *Contemporary Child Care Policy and Practice*. Basingstoke: Palgrave Macmillan.

Felson, M. (1998) *Crime and Everyday Life*. Thousand Oaks, CA: Pine Forge Press.

Figueroa, M. and Sives, A. (2002) 'Homogenous Voting, Electoral Manipulation and the "Garrison" Process in Post-Independence Jamaica', *Journal of Commonwealth and Comparative Politics*, 40 (1): 80–108.

Forrester, D., Frenz, S., O'Connell, M. and Pease, K. (1990) *The Kirkholt Burglary Prevention Project: Phase II*. London: Home Office.

Fitzgerald, M., Stockdale, J. and Hale, C. (2003) *Young People and Street Crime*. London: Youth Justice Board.

Foucault, M. (1972) *Power/Knowledge*. London: Harvester Press.

Fyvel, T. R. (1969) *The Insecure Offenders*. Harmondsworth: Penguin.

Galster, G. and Zobel, A. (1998) 'Will Dispersed Housing Programmes Reduce Social Problems in the US?', *Housing Studies*, 13 (5): 605–22.

Garland, D. (2001) *The Culture of Control*. Oxford: Oxford University Press.

Gatti, U., Angelini, F., Marengo, G., Melchiorre, N. and Sasso, M. (2005) 'An Old-fashioned Youth Gang in Genoa', in S. Decker and F. Weerman (eds) *European Street Gangs and Troublesome Youth Groups*. Lanham, MD: AltaMira Press.

Giddens, A. (1999) *The Third Way: The Renewal of Social Democracy*. Cambridge: Polity Press.

Gilroy, P. (1992) *There Ain't No Black in the Union Jack: The Cultural Politics of Race and Nation*. London: Routledge.

Gladwell, M. (2000) *The Tipping Point: How Little Things Can Make a Big Difference*. Boston, MA: Little, Brown.

Goffman, I. (1968) *Stigma: Notes on the Management of Spoiled Identity*. Harmondsworth: Penguin.

Goldson, B. (2002) 'Youth Crime, the "Parenting Deficit" and State Intervention: A Contextual Critique', *Youth Justice*, 2 (2): 82–99.

Gordon, R. (2000) 'Criminal Business Organisations, Street Gangs and "Wanna Be" Groups: A Vancouver Perspective', *Canadian Journal of Criminology and Criminal Justice*, 42 (1).

Gunst, L. (2003) *Born Fi' Dead: A Journey Through the Jamaican Posse Underworld*. New York: Holt, Rinehart and Winston.

Hagan, J. (1993) 'The Social Embeddedness of Crime and Unemployment', *Criminology*, 31: 455–91.

Hagedorn, J. (1998) *People and Folks: Gangs, Crime and the Underclass in a Rustbelt City*, 2nd edn. Chicago: Lakeview Press.

Hagedorn, J. (2007) 'Introduction: Globalisation, Gangs and Traditional Criminology', in J. Hagedorn (ed.) *Gangs in the Global City: Alternatives to Traditional Criminology*. Chicago: University of Illinois Press.

Hall, S. and Jefferson, T. (eds) (1975) *Resistance Through Rituals: Youth Subcultures in Post-War Britain*. Routledge: London.

Hall, S., Critcher, C., Jefferson, T., Clarke, J. and Roberts, B. (1978) *Policing the Crisis: Mugging, the State and Law and Order*. London: Macmillan.

Hallam, S. (2008) 'Policing in the Iron Cage: The Tensions Between the Bureaucratic Mandate and Street Level Reality', unpublished PhD thesis, University of Bedfordshire.

Hallsworth, S. (2005) *Street Crime*. Cullompton, Willan Publishing.

Hallsworth, S. and Young, T. (2004) 'Getting Real About Gangs', *Criminal Justice Matters*, 55: 12–13.

Hanley, L (2007) *Estates: An Intimate History*. London: Granta Books.

Hill, K. G., Hawkins, J. D., Catalano, R. F., Kosterman, R., Abbott, R. and Edwards, T. (1996) 'The Longitudinal Dynamics of Gang Membership and Problem Behavior: A Replication and Extension of the Denver and

Rochester Gang Studies in Seattle', paper presented at the annual meeting of the American Criminological Society, Chicago, November.

Hirschi, T. (1969) *The Causes of Delinquency*. Berkeley: University of California Press.

Hobbs, D. (1988) *Doing the Business: Entrepreneurship, the Working Class, and Detectives in the East End of London*. Oxford: Clarendon Press.

Hobbs, D. (2001) 'The Firm: Organizational Logic and Criminal Culture on a Shifting Terrain', *British Journal of Criminology*, 41: 549–60 (e-journal).

Hobbs, D. and Dunningham, C. (1998) Glocal Organised Crime: Context and Pretext', in V. Ruggiero, N. South and I. Taylor I. (eds) *The New European Criminology*. London: Routledge.

Home Office (2006) *Group Offending*. London: Home Office.

Home Office/RDS (2004) *Gun Crime*. London: Home Office.

Hope, T. (2003) 'The Crime Drop in Britain', *Community Safety Journal*, 2 (4): 32.

Hope, T. and Foster, J. (1992) 'Conflicting Forces: Changing the Dynamics of Crime and Community on a Problem Estate', *British Journal of Criminology*, 32 (4): 488–504.

Howell, J. and Egley, A. (2005) 'Moving Risk Factors into Developmental Theories of Gang Membership', *Youth Violence and Juvenile Justice*, 3 (4): 334–54.

Jephcott, P. (1954) *Some Young People: A Study of Adolescent Boys and Girls*. London: George Allen and Unwin.

Jordan, B. (2004) 'Emancipatory Social Work? Opportunity or Oxymoron', *British Journal of Social Work*, 34: 5–19.

Karstedt, S. and Farrall, S. (2007) *Law-abiding Majority? The Everyday Crimes of the Middle Classes*. London: Centre for Crime and Justice Studies, Kings College.

Katz, J. (1988) *The Seductions of Crime: The Moral and Sensual Attractions of Doing Evil*. New York: Basic Books.

Kennedy, D. (2007) 'How to Stop Young Men Shooting Each Other', presentation to the Metropolitan Police Authority.

Klein, M. (1969) 'Gang Cohesiveness, Delinquency, and a Street-Work Program', *Journal of Research in Crime and Delinquency*, 6 (2): 135–66.

Klein M. (1996) 'Gangs in the United States and Europe', *European Journal of Criminal Policy and Research*, 4 (2): 63–80.

Klein, M. (2001) 'Resolving the Eurogang Paradox', in M. Klein, H.-J. Kerner, C. Maxson and E. Weitekamp (eds) *The Eurogang Paradox: Street Gangs and Youth Groups in the USA and Europe*. Kluwer Academic Publishing.

Klein, M. and Maxson, C. (2006) *Street Gang Patterns and Policies*. Oxford: Oxford University Press.

Lahey, B., Gordon, R., Loeber, R., Stouthamer-Loeber, M. and Farrington, D. (1999) 'Boys Who Join Gangs: A Prospective Study of Predictors of First Gang Entry', *Journal of Abnormal Child Psychology*, 27 (4).

Lal, D. and Lal, S. (1995) 'Identifying Negative Gang Activities', paper presented to South Hills Area School District Association, Pittsburgh, PA.

Lal, S. (1996) 'Gang Activity at School: Prevention Strategies', in W. Schwartz (ed.) *Preventing Youth Violence in Urban Schools*, Urban Diversity Series 107. New York: Columbia University.

Lea, J. and Young, J. (1988) *What is To Be Done About Law and Order?* Harmondsworth: Penguin.

Leventhal, T. and Brooks-Gunn, J. (2001) 'Moving to Opportunity: What About the Kids?', mimeo. New York: Columbia University.

Levitt, S. and Dubner, S. (2005) *Freakonomics: A Rogue Economist Explores the Hidden Side of Everything*. London: Allen Lane.

Li, X., Stanton, B., Pack, R., Harris, C., Cottrell, L. and Burns, J. (2002) 'Risk and Protective Factors Associated with Gang Involvement Among Urban African American Adolescents', *Youth and Society*, 34 (2): 172–94.

McAra, L. (2006) 'Welfare in Crisis? Key Developments in Scottish Youth Justice', in J. Muncie and B. Goldson (eds) *Comparative Youth Justice: Critical Issues*. London: Sage.

McGahey, R. M. (1986) 'Economic Conditions, Neighbourhood Organisation and Urban Crime', in A. Reiss and M. Tonry (eds) *Communities and Crime*. Chicago: Chicago University Press.

McKinney, K. (1988) 'Juvenile Gangs: Crime and Drug Trafficking', *Juvenile Justice Bulletin* (September): 1–8.

McLagan, G. (2006) *Guns and Gangs: The Inside Story of the War on Our Streets*. London: Allison & Busby.

Mahomed, S. (2006) *Youth Gangs in Lambeth*. London: London Borough of Lambeth Community Safety Division.

Marlow, A. (2007) 'An Evaluation of the Bedfordshire Prolific and Priority Offender Project', *Community Safety Journal*, 6 (2).

Marris, P. and Rein, M. (1965) *Dilemmas of Social Reform: Poverty and Community Action in the United States*. Englewood Cliffs, NJ: Prentice Hall.

Marsh, P. and Frosdick, S. (1978) *Football Hooliganism*. Oxford: Oxford University Press.

Matza, D. (1969) *Becoming Deviant*. Englewood Cliffs, NJ: Prentice Hall.

May, T., Duffy, M., Bradley, F. and Hough, M. (2005) *Understanding Drug Selling in Communities: Insider and Outsider Trading*. York: Joseph Rowntree Foundation.

Mays, J. B. (1954) *Growing Up in the City: A Study of Juvenile Delinquency in an Urban Neighbourhood*. Liverpool: Liverpool University Press.

Messerschmidt, J. W. (1993) *Masculinities and Crime: Critique and Reconceptualization of Theory*. Oxford: Rowan and Littlefield.

Messner, S. and Rosenfeld, R. (1994) *Crime and the American Dream*. Belmont, CA: Wadsworth.

Miller, W.B. (1982) *Crime by Youth Gangs and Groups in the United States*. Washington, DC: US Department of Justice.

Mills, C. Wright (1959) *The Sociological Imagination*. Harmondsworth: Penguin.

Moore, J. (1991) *Going Down the Barrio: Homeboys and Homegirls in Change*. Philadelphia: Temple University Press.

Morgan, Harris and Burroughs (2003) *Evaluation of the Youth Inclusion Programme*. London: Youth Justice Board for England and Wales.

Morris, L. (1995) *Social Divisions: Economic Decline and Social Structural Change*. London: UCL Press.

MPS (Metropolitan Police) (2006) *The Pan-London Gang Survey*. London: Metropolitan Police.

Muncie, J. and Hughes, G. (2002) 'Modes of Youth Governance, Political Rationalities, Criminalisation and Resistance', J. Muncie and G. Hughes (eds) *Youth Justice: Critical Readings*. London: Sage.

Murphy, P., Williams, J. and Dunning, E. (1990) *Football on Trial: Spectator Violence and Development in the Football World*. London: Routledge.

Newburn, T. and Stanko, B. (1995) *Just Boys Doing Business? Men, Masculinities and Crime*. London: Routledge.

Page, D. (1993) *Building for Communities: A Study of New Housing Association Estates*. York: Joseph Rowntree Foundation.

Palmer, S. (2008) 'Solidarity and Individualism: Racial Consciousness, Self-Perception and Intra-Racial Youth Crime', unpublished PhD thesis, University of Luton.

Palmer, S. and Pitts, J. (2006) 'Othering the Brothers', *Youth and Policy*, 91.

Park, R. (1929) 'Sociology', in W. Gee (ed.) *Research in the Social Sciences*. New York: Macmillan.

Park, R., Burgess, E. and McKenzie, R. (1925) *The City: Suggestions for the Study of Human Behavior in the Urban Environment*. Chicago: University of Chicago Press.

Parker, H. (1974) *A View from the Boys*. Newton Abbot: David and Charles.

Patrick, J. (1973) *A Glasgow Gang Observed*. London: Methuen.

Pawson, R. and Tilley, N. (1997) *Realistic Evaluation*. London: Sage.

Pearson, G. (1984) *Hooligan: A History of Respectable Fears*. Basingstoke: Macmillan.

Pearson, G. (1988) *The New Heroin Users*. Oxford: Blackwell.

Pearson, G. (1993) 'The Role of Culture in the Drug Question', in M. Lader, G. Edwards and D. Drummond (eds) *The Nature of Alcohol and Drug-related Problems*. Oxford: Oxford University Press.

Pearson, G. and Hobbs, D. (2001) *Middle Market Drug Distribution*. London: Home Office.

Pearson, G. and Mungham, G. (eds) (1976) *Working Class Youth Culture.* London: Routledge and Kegan Paul.

Pettit, B. and McLanahan, S. (2001) 'Social Dimensions of Moving to Opportunity', *Poverty Research News,* 5 (1): 7–10.

Pitts, J. (2003) *The New Politics of Youth Crime: Discipline or Solidarity.* Lyme Regis: Russell House Publishing.

Pitts, J. (2006) *An Evaluation of the Lambeth X-It (Gang Desistance Programme).* London: London Borough of Lambeth.

Pitts, J. (2007a) 'Americanisation, the Third Way and the Racialization of Youth Crime and Disorder', in J. Hagedorn (ed.) *Gangs in the Global City.* Chicago: University of Illinois Press.

Pitts, J. (2007b) 'Who Cares What Works', *Youth and Policy,* 95 (Spring).

Pitts, J. (2008) *Young and Safe in Lambeth: The Deliberations of Lambeth Executive Commission on Children, Young People and Violent Crime.* London: London Borough of Lambeth.

Pitts, J. and Hope, T. (1997) 'The Local Politics of Inclusion: The State and Community Safety', *Social Policy and Administration,* 31 (5).

Pitts, J. and Porteous, D. (2005) 'Nobody Should be Alone', *European Journal of Social Work,* 8 (4): 435–50.

Power, A. and Tunstall, T. (1995) *Swimming Against the Tide: Polarisation or Progress.* York: Joseph Rowntree Foundation.

Pryce, K. (1979) *Endless Pressure: A study of West-Indian Lifestyles in Britain.* Bristol: Bristol Classical Press.

Robins, D. (1992) *Tarnished Vision: Crime and Conflict in the Inner Cities.* Oxford: Oxford University Press.

Rutter, M. and Giller, H. (1983) *Juvenile Delinquency: Trends and Perspectives.* Harmondsworth: Penguin.

Ryan, A. (2001) 'The Peer Group as a Context for the Development of Young Adolescent Motivation and Achievement', *Child Development,* 72 (4): 1135–50.

Sampson, R. and Lauritsen, L. (1994) 'Violent Victimisation and Offending: Individual, Situational and Community-level Risk Factors', in A. Reiss and J. Roth (eds) *Social Influences, Vol. 3: Understanding and Preventing Violence.* Washington, DC: National Academy Press.

Sampson, R. and Laub, J. (1993) *Crime in the Making: Pathways and Turning Points.* Cambridge, MA: Harvard University Press.

Sanders, W. (2004) 'Gang Culture and Street Crime in a London Neighbourhood', unpublished PhD thesis, London School of Economics.

Sassen, S. (2007) 'The Global City: One Setting for New Types of Gang Work and Political Culture', in J. Hagedorn (ed.) *Gangs in the Global City.* Chicago: University of Illinois Press.

Sennett, R. and Cobb, J. (1972) *The Hidden Injuries of Class.* New York: Vintage Books.

Shaw, C. and McKay, H. (1942) *Juvenile Delinquency and Urban Areas*. Chicago: University of Chicago Press.

Short, J. (1997) *Poverty, Ethnicity and Violent Crime*. Boulder, CO: Westview Press.

Short, J. and Strodtbeck, F. (1974) *Group Process and Gang Delinquency*. Chicago: University of Chicago Press.

Simon, J. (2007) 'Governing Through Crime', in L. Friedman and G. Fisher (eds) *The Crime Conundrum: Essays on Criminal Justice*. Boulder, CO: Westview Press.

Silverman, J. (1994) *Crack of Doom*. Bidford-on-Avon: Headline.

Skynner, R. (1971) 'The Minimum Sufficient Network', *Social Work Today* (August).

Smith, C. H. (1997) 'Method in the Madness: Exploring the Boundaries of Identity in Hip-Hop Performativity', *Social Identities: Journal for the Study of Race, Nation and Culture*, 3: 354–74.

Social Exclusion Unit (1998) *Bringing Britain Together: A National Strategy for Neighbourhood Renewal*, Report of Policy Action Team 12 (Young People). London: Stationery Office.

Spergel, I. (1989) 'Youth Gangs: Problem and Response, A Review of the Literature', Executive Summary, Draft, Chicago School of Social Service Administration, University of Chicago.

Spergel, I. and Curry, D. (1993) 'The National Youth Gang Survey', in A. P. Goldstein and C. R. Huff (eds) *The Gang Intervention Handbook*. Champaign, IL: Research Press.

Spergel, I. and Grossman, S. (1997) 'The Little Village Project: A Community Approach to the Gang Problem', *Social Work*, 42: 456–70.

Stelfox, P. (1998) 'Policing Lower Levels of Organised Crime in England and Wales', *The Howard Journal*, 37 (4).

Stover, D. (1986) 'A New Breed of Youth Gang is on the Prowl and a Bigger Threat Than Ever', *American School Board Journal*, 173 (8): 19–24, 35.

Sullivan, M. (1989) *Getting Paid: Youth Crime and Work in the Inner City*. Ithaca, NY: Cornell University Press.

Sutherland, E. and Cressey, D. (1966) *Principles of Criminology*. Philadelphia: J. P. Lippincott.

Suttles, G. D. (1968) *The Social Order of the Slum*. Chicago: University of Chicago Press.

Taylor, I. (1971) 'Soccer Consciousness and Soccer Hooliganism', in S. Cohen (ed.) *Images of Deviance*. Harmondsworth: Penguin.

Taylor-Gooby, P. (2003) 'The Genuinely Liberal Genuine Welfare State', paper presented at the Social Policy Association Conference, University of Teesside, 16 July.

Thornbury, T. (1998) 'Membership of Youth Gangs and Involvement in Serious and Violent Offending', in R. Loeber and D. Farrington (eds) *Serious and Violent Juvenile Offenders*. London: Sage.

Thrasher, F. (1929) *The Gang*. Chicago: University of Chicago Press.
Tursman, C. (1989) 'Safeguarding Schools Against Gang Warfare', *School Administrator*, 46 (5): 8–9, 13–15.

Valier, C. (2003) *Theories of Crime and Punishment*. London: Longman.
Vigil, D. (1987) *A Rainbow of Gangs: Street Cultures in the Mega-City*. Texas: Texas University Press.

Wacquant, L. (2004) *Deadly Symbiosis*. Cambridge: Polity Press.
Walklate, S. (1999) 'Excavating the Fear of Crime', *Theoretical Criminology*, 2(4): 403–18.
Weber, M. (1947) *The Theory of Social and Economic Organization* (trs. A.M. Henderson and T. Parsons). New York: The Free Press.
West, D. and Farrington, D. (1973) *Who Becomes Delinquent?* London: Heinemann.
Whyte, W.F. (1943) *Street Corner Society: The Social Structure of an Italian Slum*. Chicago: University of Chicago Press.
Wikstrom, T. and Loeber, R. (1997) 'Individual Risk Factors, Neighbourhood SES and Juvenile Offending', in M. Tonry (ed.) *The Handbook of Crime and Punishment*. New York: Oxford University Press.
Willmott, P. (1966) *Adolescent Boys in East London*. Harmondsworth: Penguin.
Wilson, W. J. (1987) *The Truly Disadvantaged: The Inner City, the Underclass and Public Policy*. Chicago: University of Chicago Press.
Wright, R., Brookman, F. and Bennett, T. (2006) 'The Foreground Dynamics of Street Robbery in Britain', *British Journal of Criminology*, 46 (1): 1–15.

Yablonsky, L. (1962) *The Violent Gang*. Harmondsworth: Penguin.
Young, J. (1999) *The Exclusive Society: Social Exclusion, Crime and Difference in Late Modernity*. London: Sage.
Young, J. (2007) *The Vertigo of Late Modernity*. London: Sage.
Young, J. and Matthews, R. (1992) *Re-thinking Criminology: The Realist Debate*. London: Sage.
Youth Justice Board (2007) *Groups, Gangs and Weapons*. London: Youth Justice Board.

Zorbaugh, H. W. (1929) *The Gold Coast and the Slum: A Sociological Study of Chicago's North Side*. Chicago: Chicago University Press.

Index